A

MANUAL

FOR USE AT

FUNERALS

CONSISTING OF

SCRIPTURE READINGS, POEMS, AND PROSE
SELECTIONS FROM VARIOUS SOURCES

Staples C. J.

————————

BOSTON
GEO. H. ELLIS, 141 FRANKLIN STREET
1892

CONTENTS.

PREFACE.

THIS manual has been compiled in hope of assisting ministers and laymen in the task of preparing and conducting funeral services. Each occasion of bereavement is different from all others, and each funeral service requires special preparation. While, therefore, a "general service," containing selections appropriate to the majority of occasions, has been arranged, it is offered with the idea of being shortened and supplemented according to the judgment of the minister and the special circumstances that may arise. For this purpose we have brought together all passages of scripture which seemed appropriate, and have grouped them under various headings, so that anyone, with comparatively little trouble, can form the special service he needs.

While the manual is compiled with reference to its use at funerals, it is hoped that the selections here made, of prose and poetry, may be of service, also, as devotional readings, in the sick room or elsewhere.

The choice of poems was not an easy task. Many favorites will be missed, no doubt, and it cannot be hoped that the poems given will be of equal value to all. We have selected, as far as possible, those which have already proved their fitness for such uses.

With very few exceptions, the poems are given without change, since every clergyman will feel at liberty to make his own alterations, if they are deemed necessary. For lack of space, however, many of the poems have been shortened by the omission of stanzas irrelevant to funeral occasions. Such will be found marked with a star in the index of first lines. We have not printed hymns easily accessible in the Revised Hymn and Tune Book of the American Unitarian Association, though many of them are specially appropriate.

A supplementary list of poems which may be found serviceable with slight changes, has been added. Selections from extra-biblical scriptures, and from various writers, ancient and modern, have also been made, in the belief that they will be useful, if not as readings in the service itself, then as suggestive thoughts. A few prayers, original and selected, are given for the use of laymen called upon to conduct funeral services.

The compilers are indebted to the kindness of many friends for the suggestions they have made and the assistance they have given. Special acknowledgment is due to Messrs. Houghton, Mifflin & Co., Roberts Brothers, and others, for their courtesy in permitting the use of copyright poems.

CHRISTOPHER R. ELIOT.
CHARLES J. STAPLES.

I.

ALMIGHTY God, we come to thee because we need thee. Without thee we are poor and weak, and with thee we can be brave and strong. We bow ourselves before thy will. We yield ourselves to thy law. Thou sendest forth thy Spirit, we are created; thou takest away our breath, we die and return to the dust. In death as in life, in sorrow as in joy, thou art waiting to bless us, if we will but turn to thee. Thou dost gird and guide us, though we know it not; and the shadow with which thou darkenest our way is but the shadow of thy close-approaching and over-brooding presence.

Help us to find thee thus this day. Lead us from our weakness to thy strength, and from our ignorance to thy wisdom, and give to us the peace and confidence which walks in the darkness even as in the light. It is thou who dost take to thyself the life of this, thy servant. Help us to say and to believe that it is well, — well with the life which seems to go away, because it finds thy rest and peace, and well for us who stay, because of tender memories and Christian hopes. In the midst of grief and solitude give to us the prayer of gratitude and praise. As we perceive that the things which are seen are temporal, so much the more may we find that the things which are unseen are eternal. Strengthen in us that immortal hope which is ours in the discipleship of Jesus. Make us know that if our earthly house be dissolved, we have a building of God, a house not made with hands, eternal in the heavens; and, amid the sufferings of this present time, unveil to us the things which eye hath not seen, but which God hath prepared for them that love him.

Sanctify thus to these hearts the sorrow which thou

dost call upon them to bear. May they hear that voice
which says, " Blessed are they that mourn, for they
shall be comforted." As they walk through the valley
of the shadow of death, may thy rod and staff support
them, and may they be grateful for that Eternal Love
which summons souls to rest from their labors, and dost
permit them to enter into thy peace. Send us all back
to our lives more eager to serve thee, and more inclined
to love thee, as though in this mysterious presence we
had learned to know the deeper meaning and responsi-
bility of life. Amid the changes of this world make us
strong and calm, because we rest in thee, and finally
persuade us that neither death nor life, nor things present,
nor things to come, shall be able to separate us from the
love of God which is in Christ Jesus, our Lord. *Amen.*

F. G. P.

II.

O FATHER, we would not forget thy benefits. For
life we thank thee; the throbbing life of Nature; the
quick-beating pulse of human hearts, the swift flight of
the spirit's prayer, the life eternal. For love we thank
thee; that love which, from childhood onward, has been
ours, blessing us, saving us, creating us anew. For hope
we thank thee, and for light; for all that quickens faith;
for the mind and heart of Christ; for the in-flowing of
thy Spirit.

O God, we call thee, and thou art here. We are not
strong; grant us thy strength. We cannot see; grant
us thy light. We do not know the way; lead us, O
Father, by thy Spirit. We falter, we wander, we dare
not speak; only teach thou us to pray. So, in us, and
through us, may thy kingdom come, and thy will be
done. *Amen.*   *C. R. E.*

. LIFE.

The ungodly said, reasoning with themselves, but not aright, Our life is short and tedious, and in the death of a man there is no remedy : neither was there any man known to have returned from the grave. For we are born at all adventure : and we shall be hereafter as though we had never been : for the breath in our nostrils is as smoke, and a little spark in the moving of our heart : which being extinguished, our body shall be turned into ashes, and our spirit shall vanish as the soft air, and our name shall be forgotten in time, and no man shall have our works in remembrance, and our life shall pass away as the trace of a cloud, and shall be dispersed as a mist, that is driven away with the beams of the sun, and overcome with the heat thereof. For our time is a very shadow that passeth away ; and after our end there is no returning : for it is fast sealed, so that no man cometh again.   Come on therefore, let us enjoy the good things that are present : and let us speedily use the creatures like as in youth. [Let us fill ourselves with costly wine and ointments : and] let no flower of the spring pass by us : let us crown ourselves with rosebuds, before they be withered : [et none of us go without his part of our voluptuousness : let us leave tokens of our joyfulness in every place :] for this is our portion, and our lot is this.   Such things they did imagine, and were deceived : for their own wickedness hath blinded them. As for the mysteries of God, they knew them not : neither hoped they for the wages of righteousness, nor discerned a reward for blameless souls. For God created man to be immortal, and made him to be an image of his own eternity. [*Wisdom ii.*]

The souls of the righteous are in the hand of God, and there shall no torment touch them. In the sight of the unwise they seemed to die: and their departure is taken for misery, and their going from us to be utter destruction: but they are in peace. For though they be punished in the sight of men, yet is their hope full of immortality. And having been a little chastised, they shall be greatly rewarded: for God proved them, and found them worthy for himself. As gold in the furnace hath he tried them, and received them as a burnt offering. [*Wisdom iii.*]

To every thing there is a season, and a time to every purpose under the heaven: a time to be born, and a time to die; a time to plant, and a time to pluck up that which is planted; a time to kill, and a time to heal; a time to break down, and a time to build up; a time to weep, and a time to laugh; a time to mourn, and a time to dance; a time to rend, and a time to sew; a time to keep silence, and a time to speak; a time to love, and a time to hate; a time of war, and a time of peace.   What profit hath he that worketh in that wherein he laboreth? I have seen the travail, which God hath given to the sons of men to be exercised in it. He hath made every thing beautiful in his time: also he hath set the world in their heart, so that no man can find out the work that God maketh from the beginning to the end. I know that there is no good in them, but for a man to rejoice, and to do good in his life. And also that every man enjoy the good of all flower fadeth : but the word of our God shall stand forever. [*Isa. xl.*]

A man's heart deviseth his way : but the Lord directeth his steps. [*Prov. xvi.*] [For what man is he that can know the counsel of God? or who can think what the will of the Lord is?] For the thoughts of mortal men are miserable, and our devices are but uncertain. For the corruptible body presseth down the soul, and the earthy tabernacle weigheth down the mind that museth upon many things. And hardly do we guess aright at things that are upon earth, and with labor do we find the things that are before us : but the things that are in heaven who hath searched out? And thy counsel who hath known, except thou give wisdom and send thy Holy Spirit from above? For so the ways of them which lived on the earth were reformed, and men were taught the things that are pleasing unto thee, and were saved through wisdom. [*Wisdom ix.*]

Lord, make me to know mine end, and the measure of my days, what it is; that I may know how frail I am. Behold, thou hast made my days as a handbreadth ; and mine age is as nothing before thee : verily every man at his best state is altogether vanity. Surely every man walketh in a vain show : surely they are disquieted in vain : he heapeth up riches, and knoweth not who shall gather them. And now, Lord, what wait I for? my hope is in thee. [Deliver me from all my transgressions. I was dumb, I opened not my mouth ; because thou didst it. Remove thy stroke away from me : I am consumed by the blow of thine hand.] When thou with rebukes dost correct man for iniquity, thou makest his beauty to consume away like a moth: surely every man is vanity. Hear my prayer, O Lord, and give ear unto my cry: hold not thy peace at my tears: for I am a stranger with thee, and a sojourner, as all my fathers were. O spare me, that I may recover strength, before I go hence, and be no more. [*Ps. xxxix.*]

THE LIFE OF THE SPIRIT.

There is a spirit in man: and the inspiration of the Almighty giveth them understanding. [*Job xxxii.*]

Jesus said unto her, I am the resurrection, and the life: he that believeth in me, though he were dead, yet shall he live: and whosoever liveth and believeth in me shall never die. [*John xi.*] Verily, verily, I say unto you, He that heareth my word, and believeth on him that sent me, hath eternal life, and shall not come into condemnation; but is passed from death unto life. [*John v.*] For bodily exercise profiteth little: but godliness is profitable unto all things, having promise of the life that now is, and of that which is to come. [*1 Tim. iv.*] In the way of righteousness is life; and in the pathway thereof there is no death. [*Prov. xii.*]

Labor not for the meat which perisheth, but for that meat which endureth unto eternal life, which the Son of man shall give unto you: for him hath God the Father sealed. Verily, verily, I say unto you, Moses gave you not that bread from heaven: but my Father giveth you the true bread from heaven. For the bread of God is he

which cometh down from heaven, and giveth life unto
the world. Then said they unto him, Lord, evermore
give us this bread. And Jesus said unto them, I am the
bread of life : he that cometh to me shall never hunger ;
and he that believeth on me shall never thirst. Verily,
verily, I say unto you, He that believeth on me hath
everlasting life. I am that bread of life. Your fathers
did eat manna in the wilderness, and are dead. This is
the bread which cometh down from heaven, that a man
may eat thereof, and not die. [*John vi.*]

Jesus answered and said unto her, Whosoever drinketh
of this water shall thirst again : but whosoever drinketh
of the water that I shall give him shall never thirst; but
the water that I shall give him shall be in him a well of
water springing up into eternal life. [*John iv.*]

Behold I come quickly ; and my reward is with me, to
give every man according as his works shall be. I am
Alpha and Omega, the beginning and the end, the first
and the last. Blessed are they that do his commandments,
that they may have right to the tree of life, and may enter
in through the gates into the city. And the Spirit and
the bride say, Come. And let him that heareth say,
Come. And let him that is athirst come. And whosoever will, let him take the water of life freely. [*Rev. xxii.*]

THE DEEP WATERS.

Save me, O God ; for the waters are come in unto my
soul. I am come into deep waters, where the floods
overflow me. [*Ps. lxix.*] The floods have lifted up, O

Lord, the floods have lifted up their voice; the floods lift up their waves. [*Ps. xciii.*]   Deep calleth unto deep at the noise of thy waterspouts: all thy waves and thy billows have gone over me. [*Ps. xlii.*]   The Lord on high is mightier than the noise of many waters, yea, than the mighty waves of the sea. [*Ps. xciii.*]

O Lord God of my salvation, I have cried day and night before thee: let my prayer come before thee: incline thine ear unto my cry: for my soul is full of troubles: (and my life draweth nigh unto the grave) I am counted with them that go down into the pit: I am as a man that hath no strength: mine eye mourneth by reason of affliction: Lord, I have called daily upon thee, I have stretched out my hands unto thee. Wilt thou shew wonders to the dead? shall the dead arise and praise thee? Shall thy loving-kindness be declared in the grave? or thy faithfulness in destruction? Shall thy wonders be known in the dark? and thy righteousness in the land of forgetfulness? But unto thee have I cried, O Lord; and in the morning shall my prayer prevent thee. Lord, why castest thou off my soul? Why hidest thou thy face from me? [*Ps. lxxxviii.*] Hide not thy face from thy servant; for I am in trouble: hear me speedily. [*Ps. lxix.*]

Woe is me for my hurt! my wound is grievous: but I said, Truly this is a grief, and I must bear it. My tabernacle is spoiled, and all my cords are broken: my children are gone forth of me, and they are not: there is none to stretch forth my tent any more, and to set up my curtains. O Lord, I know that the way of man is not in himself: it is not in man that walketh to direct his steps. O Lord, correct me, but with judgment: not in thine anger, lest thou bring me to nothing. [*Jer. x.*]

Is it nothing to you, all ye that pass by? behold, and see if there be any sorrow like unto my sorrow, which is done unto me, wherewith the Lord hath afflicted me. [*Lam. i.*] I am so troubled that I cannot speak. I have considered the days of old, the years of ancient times. I call to remembrance my song in the night: I commune with mine own heart: and my spirit made diligent search. Will the Lord cast off for ever? and will he be favorable no more? Is his mercy clean gone for ever? doth his promise fail for evermore? Hath God forgotten to be gracious? hath he in anger shut up his tender mercies? And I said, This is my infirmity: but I will remember the years of the right hand of the Most High. [*Ps. lxxvii.*]

It is better to go to the house of mourning than to go to the house of feasting: for that is the end of all men; and the living will lay it to his heart. Sorrow is better than laughter: for by the sadness of the countenance the heart is made better. The heart of the wise is in the house of mourning: but the heart of fools is in the house of mirth. In the day of prosperity be joyful, but in the day of adversity consider: God also hath set the one over against the other, to the end that man should find nothing after him. [*Eccl. vii.*]

Although affliction cometh not forth of the dust, neither doth trouble spring out of the ground; yet man is born unto trouble, as the sparks fly upward. [*Job v.*]

SUDDEN DEATH.

Boast not thyself of to-morrow ; for thou knowest not what a day may bring forth. [*Prov. xxvii.*]   But, be-loved) be not ignorant of this one thing, that one day is with the Lord as a thousand years, and a thousand years as one day.   The Lord is not slack concerning his prom-ise, as some men count slackness : but is long-suffering to us-ward, not willing that any should perish, but that all should come to repentance.   But the day of the Lord will come as a thief in the night ; in the which the heav-ens shall pass away with a great noise, and the elements shall melt with fervent heat, the earth also and the works that are therein shall be burned up.   Seeing then that all these things shall be dissolved, what manner of persons ought ye to be in all holy conversation and godliness, looking for and hasting unto the coming of the day of God, wherein the heavens being on fire shall be dissolved, and the elements shall melt with fervent heat?   Never-theless we, according to his promise, look for new heav-ens and a new earth, wherein dwelleth righteousness. Wherefore, beloved, seeing that ye look for such things, be diligent that ye may be found of him in peace, with-out spot, and blameless. [*2 Pet. iii.*]

But of that day and hour knoweth no man, no, not the angels of heaven, but my Father only.   But as the days of Noah were, so shall also the coming of the Son of man be. For as in the days that were before the flood they were eating and drinking, marrying, and giving in marriage, until the day that Noah entered into the ark, and knew not until the flood came, and took them all away ; so

shall also the coming of the Son of man be. Then
shall two be in the field; the one shall be taken, and
the other left. Two women shall be grinding at the
mill; the one shall be taken, and the other left. Watch
therefore; for ye know not what hour your Lord
doth come. But know this, that if the goodman of the
house had known in what watch the thief would come,
he would have watched, and would not have suffered his
house to be broken up. Therefore be ye also ready: for
in such an hour as ye think not the Son of man cometh.
Who then is a faithful and wise servant, whom his lord
hath made ruler over his household, to give them meat in
due season? Blessed is that servant, whom his lord
when he cometh shall find so doing. Verily I say unto
you, that he shall make him ruler over all his goods.
[*Matt. xxiv.*]

Go to now, ye that say, To-day or to-morrow, we will
go into such a city, and continue there a year, and buy
and sell, and get gain. Whereas ye know not what shall
be on the morrow. For what is your life? It is even a
vapor, that appeareth for a little time, and then vanisheth
away. [*Jas. iv.*] Now my days are swifter than a post:
they flee away: they are passed away as the swift ships.
[*Job ix.*] My days are swifter than a weaver's shuttle.
[*Job vii.*] As the Lord liveth and as thy soul liveth,
there is but a step between me and death. [*1 Sam. xx.*]
Yet I will say of the Lord, He is my refuge and my for-
tress: my God; in him will I trust. Thou shalt not be
afraid for the terror by night; nor for the arrow that flieth
by day; nor for the pestilence that walketh in darkness;
nor for the destruction that wasteth at noonday. For he

shall give his angels charge over thee, to keep thee in all thy ways. [*Ps. xci.*]

I must work the works of nim that sent me, while it is day : the night cometh, when no man can work. [*John ix.*] Watch ye therefore : for ye know not when the master of the house cometh, at even, or at midnight, or at the cockcrowing, or in the morning : lest coming suddenly he find you sleeping. And what I say unto you I say unto all, Watch. [*Mark xiii.*]

TRIAL AND SUFFERING.

Blessed is the man that endureth temptation : for when he is tried, he shall receive the crown of life, which the Lord hath promised to them that love him. [*Jas. i.*]

I heard, but I understood not : then said I, O my Lord, what shall be the end of these things? And he said, Go thy way, Daniel : for the words are closed up and sealed till the time of the end. Many shall be puri- fied, and made white, and tried ; but the wicked shall do wickedly : and none of the wicked shall understand ; but the wise shall understand. Blessed is he that waiteth. But go thou thy way till the end be : for thou shalt rest, and stand in thy lot at the end of the days. [*Dan. xii.*]

Then came to him the mother of Zebedee's children with her sons, worshipping him, and desiring a certain thing of him. And he said unto her, What wilt thou ? She saith unto him, Grant that these my two sons may sit, the one on thy right hand, and the other on the left, in thy kingdom.   But Jesus answered and said, Ye know not what ye ask.   Are ye able to drink of the cup that I shall drink of, and to be baptized with the baptism that I am baptized with?   They say unto him, We are able. And he saith unto them, Ye shall drink indeed of my cup, and be baptized with the baptism that I am baptized with : but to sit on my right hand, and on my left, is not mine to give, but it shall be given to them for whom it is prepared of my Father. [*Matt. xx.*] For we are laborers together with God : ye are God's husbandry, ye are God's building.   According to the grace of God which is given unto me, as a wise masterbuilder, I have laid the foundation, and another buildeth thereon.   But let every man take heed how he buildeth thereupon.   For other foundation can no man lay than that is laid, which is Jesus Christ.   Now if any man build upon this foundation gold, silver, precious stones, wood, hay, stubble ; every man's work shall be made manifest : for the day shall declare it, because it shall be revealed by fire ; and the fire shall try every man's work of what sort it is.   If any man's work abide which he hath built thereupon, he shall receive a reward.   If any man's work shall be burned, he shall suffer loss : but he himself shall be saved ; yet so as by fire.   Know ye not that ye are the temple of God, and that the spirit of God dwelleth in you? If any man defile the temple of God, him shall God destroy ; for the temple of God is holy, which temple ye are. [1 *Cor. iii.*]

Behold, I come quickly : hold that fast which thou hast, that no man take thy crown.   Him that overcometh will I make a pillar in the temple of my God, and he shall go no more out : and I will write upon him the name of my God, and the name of the city of my God, which is new

Jerusalem, which cometh down out of heaven from my God : and I will write upon him my new name. [*Rev. iii.*] To him that overcometh will I give to eat of the tree of life, which is in the midst of the ~~~ "~~~ ~~~~~ [*Rev. ii.*]

                     ~~~ correcteth:

               of the Al-

  Wherefore   up: he

not as in my   He shall deliver

absence, wo   shall no evil

trembling: f   thee from death:

will and to d   Thou shalt

                     neither shalt thou

THE WILL OF GOD.

Then cometh Jesus with them unto a place called Geth-semane, and saith unto the disciples, Sit ye here, while I go and pray yonder. And he went a little further, and fell on his face, and prayed, saying, O my Father, if it be possible, let this cup pass from me : nevertheless, not as I will, but as thou wilt. And he cometh unto the disciples, and findeth them asleep, and saith unto Peter, What, could ye not watch with me one hour? Watch and pray, that ye enter not into temptation : the spirit indeed is willing, but the flesh is weak. He went away again the second time, and prayed, saying, O my Father, if this cup may not pass away from me, except I drink it, thy will be done. [*Matt. xxvi.*]

    There hath no temptation taken you but such as is common to man : but God is faithful, who will not suffer you to be tempted above that ye are able ; but will with be to fearful hearts, and faint hands, and the sinner that goeth two ways! Woe unto him that is faint-hearted! for he believeth not; therefore shall he not be defended. Woe unto you that have lost patience! and what will ye do when the Lord shall visit you? They that fear the Lord will not disobey his word; and they that love him will keep his ways. They that fear the Lord will seek that which is well-pleasing unto him; and they that love him shall be filled with the law. They that fear the Lord will prepare their hearts, and humble their souls in his sight, saying, We will fall into the hands of the Lord, and not into the hands of men: for as his majesty is, so is his mercy. [*Ecclus ii.*]

ASPIRATION.

Unto thee, O Lord, do I lift up my soul. O my God, I trust in thee: turn thee unto me, and have mercy upon me; for I am desolate and afflicted. The troubles of my heart are enlarged: O bring thou me out of my distresses. Look upon mine affliction and my pain: and forgive all my sins. O keep my soul, and deliver me: for I put my trust in thee. [*Ps. xxv.*]

Out of the depths have I cried unto thee, O Lord. Lord, hear my voice: let thine ears be attentive to the voice of my supplications. If thou, Lord, shouldest mark iniquities, O Lord, who shall stand? But there is forgiveness with thee, that thou mayest be feared. I wait for the Lord, my soul doth wait, and in his word do I hope. My soul waiteth for the Lord more than they that watch for the morning: yea, more than they that watch for the morning. Let Israel hope in the Lord: for with the Lord there is mercy, and with him is plenteous redemption. And he shall redeem Israel from all his iniquities. [*Ps. cxxx.*]

Have mercy upon me, O God, according to thy loving-kindness: according unto the multitude of thy tender mercies blot out my transgressions. Wash me thoroughly from mine iniquity, and cleanse me from my sin. Create in me a clean heart, O God; and renew a right spirit within me. Cast me not away from thy presence; and take not thy Holy Spirit from me. Restore unto me the joy of thy salvation; and uphold me with thy free Spirit. The sacrifices of God are a broken spirit: a broken and a contrite heart, O God, thou wilt not despise. [*Ps. li.*]

Hear my cry, O God; attend unto my prayer. From the end of the earth will I cry unto thee, when my heart is overwhelmed: lead me to the rock that is higher than I. For thou hast been a shelter for me, and I will trust in the covert of thy wings. [*Ps. lxi.*] Be merciful unto me, O God, be merciful unto me: for my soul trusteth in thee: yea, in the shadow of thy wings will I make my refuge, until these calamities be overpast) [*Ps. lvii.*] O send out thy light and thy truth: let them lead me; let them bring me unto thy holy hill, and to thy tabernacles. [*Ps. xliii.*] Whom have I in heaven but thee? and there is none upon earth that I desire besides thee. My flesh and my heart faileth: but God is the strength of my heart, and my portion for ever. [*Ps. lxxiii.*]

I know thy works, and charity, and service, and faith, and thy patience, and thy works; and the last to be more than the first. [*Rev. ii.*] Well done, thou good and faithful servant: thou hast been faithful over a few things, I will make thee ruler over many things: enter thou into the joy of thy Lord. [*Matt. xxv.*]

Blessed is the man that walketh not in the counsel of the ungodly, nor standeth in the way of sinners, nor sitteth in the seat of the scornful. But his delight is in the law of the Lord; and in his law doth he meditate day and night. And he shall be like a tree planted by the rivers of water, that bringeth forth his fruit in his season; his leaf also shall not wither; and whatsoever he doeth shall prosper. [*Ps. i.*]

What things were gain to me, those I counted loss for Christ. Yea doubtless, and I count all things but loss for the excellency of the knowledge of Christ Jesus my Lord: for whom I have suffered the loss of all things, and do count them but refuse, that I may win Christ, and be found in him, not having mine own righteousness, which is of the law, but that which is through the faith of Christ, the righteousness which is of God by faith: that I may know him, and the power of his resurrection, and the fellowship of his sufferings, being made conformable unto his death; if by any means I might attain unto the resurrection of the dead. Not as though I had already attained, either were already perfect: but I follow after, if that I may apprehend that for which also I am apprehended of Christ Jesus. Brethren, I count not myself to have apprehended: but this one thing I do, forgetting those things which are behind, and reaching

forth unto those things which are before, I press toward
the mark for the prize of the high calling of God in
Christ Jesus. [*Phil. iii.*]

Finally, brethren, whatsoever things are true, whatsoever things are honest, whatsoever things are just,
whatsoever things are pure, whatsoever things are lovely,
whatsoever things are of good report; if there be
any virtue, and if there be any praise, think on these
things. [*Phil. iv.*] For the memorial of virtue is immortal: because it is known with God, and with men.
When it is present, men take example at it; and when
it is gone, they desire it: it weareth a crown, and tri-
umpheth for ever, having gotten the victory, striving for
undefiled rewards. [*Wisdom iv.*]

Let us hear the conclusion of the whole matter: fear
God, and keep his commandments: for this is the whole
duty of man. For God shall bring every work into
judgment, with every secret thing, whether it be good,
or whether it be evil. [*Eccl. xii.*]

WISDOM AND WORTH.

Know ye not that there is a prince and a great man
fallen this day in Israel? [*2 Sam. iii.*] [For, behold,
the Lord, the Lord of hosts, doth take away from Jerusalem and from Judah the stay and the staff, the whole
stay of bread, and the whole stay of water, the mighty
man, and the man of war, the judge, and the prophet,
and the prudent, and the ancient, the captain of fifty,
and the honorable man, and the counsellor, and the cun-

my nest, and I shall multiply my days as the sand. My root was spread out by the waters, and the dew lay all night upon my branch. My glory was fresh in me, and my bow was renewed in my hand. Unto me men gave ear, and waited, and kept silence at my counsel. After my words they spake not again; and my speech dropped upon them. And they waited for me as for the rain; and they opened their mouth wide as for the latter rain. If I laughed on them, they believed it not: and the light of my countenance they cast not down. I chose out their way, and sat chief, and dwelt as a king in the army, as one that comforteth the mourners. [*Job xxix.*]

Blessed be the name of God for ever and ever: for wisdom and might are his: and he changeth the times and the seasons: he removeth kings, and setteth up kings: he giveth wisdom unto the wise, and knowledge to them that know understanding: he revealeth the deep and secret things: he knoweth what is in the darkness, and the light dwelleth with him. [*Dan. ii.*]

He that giveth his mind to the law of the Most High, and is occupied in the meditation thereof, will seek out the wisdom of all the ancient, and be occupied in prophecies. He will keep the sayings of the renowned men: and where subtile parables are, he will be there also. He will seek out the secrets of grave sentences, and be conversant in dark parables. He shall serve among great men, and appear before princes: he will travel through strange countries; for he hath tried the good and the evil among men. He will give his heart to resort early to the Lord that made him, and will pray before the Most

High,[and will open his mouth in prayer, and make supplication for his sins.] When the great Lord will, he shall be filled with the spirit of understanding: he shall pour out wise sentences, and give thanks unto the Lord in his prayer. He shall direct his counsel and knowledge, and in his secrets shall he meditate. He shall shew forth that which he hath learned, and shall glory in the law of the covenant of the Lord. Many shall commend his understanding; and so long as the world endureth, it shall not be blotted out; his memorial shall not depart away, and his name shall live from generation to generation. Nations shall shew forth his wisdom, and the congregation shall declare his praise. If he die, he shall leave a greater name than a thousand: and if he live, he shall increase it. [*Ecclus. xxxix.*]

The fear of the Lord is the beginning of wisdom: and the knowledge of the Holy One is understanding. [*Prov. ix.*] And unto man he said, Behold, the fear of the Lord, that is wisdom; and to depart from evil is understanding. [*Job xxviii.*]

Happy is the man that findeth wisdom, and the man that getteth understanding: for the merchandise of it is better than the merchandise of silver, and the gain thereof than fine gold. She is more precious than rubies: and all the things thou canst desire are not to be compared unto her. Length of days is in her right hand; and in her left hand riches and honor. Her ways are ways of pleasantness, and all her paths are peace. She is a tree of life to them that lay hold upon her; and happy is every one that retaineth her. My son, keep sound wisdom and discretion: so shall they be life unto thy soul, and grace to thy neck. Then shalt thou walk in thy way safely, and thy foot shall not stumble. When thou liest down, thou shalt not be afraid: yea, thou shalt lie down, and thy sleep shall be sweet. Be not afraid of sudden fear, neither of the desolation of the wicked, when it cometh. For the Lord shall be thy confidence, and shall keep thy foot from being taken. [*Prov. iii.*]

Hear, ye children, the instruction of a father, and attend to know understanding. For I give you good doctrine, forsake ye not my law. For I was my father's son, tender and only beloved in the sight of my mother. He taught me also, and said unto me, Let thine heart retain my words: keep my commandments, and live. Get wisdom, get understanding: forget it not; neither decline from the words of my mouth. Forsake her not, and she shall preserve thee: love her, and she shall keep thee. Wisdom is the principal thing; therefore get wisdom: and with all thy getting get understanding. Exalt her, and she shall promote thee: she shall bring thee to honor, when thou dost embrace her. She shall give to thine head an ornament of grace: a crown of glory shall she deliver to thee. Hear, O my son, and receive my sayings; and the years of thy life shall be many. I have taught thee in the way of wisdom; I have led thee in right paths. When thou goest, thy steps shall not be straitened; and when thou runnest, thou shalt not stumble. Take fast hold of instruction; let her not go: keep her; for she is thy life. [*Prov. iv.*]

For wisdom, which is the worker of all things, taught

me: for in her is an understanding spirit, holy, one only, manifold, subtile, lively, clear, undefiled, plain, not subject to hurt, loving the thing that is good, quick, which cannot be letted, ready to do good, kind to man, steadfast, sure, free from care, having all power, over-seeing all things, and going through all understanding, pure, and most subtile, spirits. For wisdom is more moving than any motion: she passeth and goeth through all things by reason of her pureness. For she is the breath of the power of God, and a pure influence flow-ing from the glory of the Almighty: therefore can no defiled thing fall into her. For she is the brightness of the everlasting light, the unspotted mirror of the power of God, and the image of his goodness. And being but one, she can do all things: and remaining in her she maketh all things new: and in all ages entering into holy souls, she maketh them friends of God, and proph-ets. For God loveth none but him that dwelleth with wisdom. For she is more beautiful than the sun, and above all the order of the stars: being compared with the light, she is found before it. For after this cometh night: but vice shall not prevail against wisdom. [*Wisdom vii.*]

Unto you therefore, O kings, do I speak, that ye may learn wisdom, and not fall away. For they that keep holiness holily shall be judged holy: and they that have learned such things shall find what to answer. Where-fore set your affection upon my words; desire them, and ye shall be instructed. Wisdom is glorious, and never fadeth away: yea, she is easily seen of them that love her, and found of such as seek her. Whoso seeketh her early shall have no great travail: for he shall find her sitting at his doors. To think therefore upon her is perfection of wisdom : and whoso watcheth for her shall quickly be without care. For she goeth about seeking such as are worthy of her, sheweth herself favorably unto them in the ways and meeteth them in every thought. For the very true beginning of her is the desire of discipline, and the care of discipline is love ; and love is the keeping of her laws ; and the giving heed unto her laws is the assurance of incorruption ; and incorruption maketh us near unto God : therefore the desire of wisdom bringeth to a kingdom. [*Wisdom vi.*]

And the child Samuel ministered unto the Lord before Eli. And the word of the Lord was precious in those days ; there was no open vision. And it came to pass at that time, when Eli was laid down in his place, and his eyes began to wax dim, that he could not see ; and ere the lamp of God went out in the temple of the Lord, where the ark of God was, and Samuel was laid down to sleep ; that the Lord called Samuel : and he answered, Here am I. And he ran unto Eli, and said, Here am I ; for thou calledst me. And he said, I called not ; lie down again. And he went and lay down. And the Lord called yet again, Samuel. And Samuel arose and went to Eli, and said, Here am I ; for thou didst call me. And he answered, I called not, my son ; lie down again. And the Lord called Samuel again the third time. And he arose and went to Eli, and said, Here am I ; for thou didst call me. And Eli perceived that the Lord had called the child. Therefore Eli said unto Samuel, Go, lie down ; and it shall be, if he call thee,

that thou shalt say, Speak, Lord; for thy servant heareth.
So Samuel went and lay down in his place. And the
Lord came, and stood, and called as at other times, Samuel, Samuel. Then Samuel answered, Speak; for thy
servant heareth. [*1 Sam. iii.*]

How beautiful upon the mountains are the feet of him
that bringeth good tidings, that publisheth peace; that
bringeth good tidings of good, that publisheth salvation;
that saith unto Zion, Thy God reigneth! [*Isa. lii.*]

Behold my servant, whom I uphold; mine elect, in
whom my soul delighteth; I have put my Spirit upon
him: he shall bring forth judgment to the Gentiles. He
shall not cry, nor lift up, nor cause his voice to be heard
in the street. A bruised reed shall he not break, and the
smoking flax shall he not quench: he shall bring forth
judgment unto truth. He shall not fail nor be discour-
aged, till he have set judgment in the earth: and the
isles shall wait for his law. Thus saith God the Lord,
he that created the heavens, and stretched them out; he
that spread forth the earth, and that which cometh out
of it; he that giveth breath unto the people upon it, and
spirit to them that walk therein: I the Lord have called
thee in righteousness, and will hold thine hand, and will
keep thee, and give thee for a covenant of the people,
for a light of the Gentiles; to open the blind eyes, to
bring out the prisoners from the prison, and them that
sit in darkness out of the prison house. [*Isa. xlii.*]

The spirit of the Lord God is upon me; because the
Lord hath anointed me to preach good tidings unto the
meek; he hath sent me to bind up the broken-hearted,

PATIENCE.

Therefore being justified by faith, we have peace with God through our Lord Jesus Christ: by whom also we have access by faith into this grace wherein we stand, and rejoice in hope of the glory of God. And not only so, but we glory in tribulations also; knowing that tribulation worketh patience; and patience, experience; and experience, hope: and hope maketh not ashamed; because the love of God is shed abroad in our hearts by the Holy Spirit which is given unto us. [*Rom. v.*] For this is thankworthy, if a man for conscience toward God endure grief, suffering wrongfully. For what glory is it, if, when ye be buffeted for your faults, ye shall take it patiently? but if, when ye do well, and suffer for it, ye take it patiently, this is acceptable with God. For even hereunto were ye called: because Christ also suffered for you, leaving you an example, that ye should follow his steps. [*1 Peter ii.*]

We then, as workers together with him, beseech you also that ye receive not the grace of God in vain. But in all things approving ourselves as the ministers of God, in much patience, in afflictions, in necessities, in distresses, in stripes, in imprisonments, in tumults, in labors, in watchings, in fastings; by pureness, by knowledge, by long-suffering, by kindness, by the Holy Spirit, by love unfeigned, by the word of truth, by the power of God, by the armor of righteousness on the right hand and on the left, by honor and dishonor, by evil report and good report: as deceivers, and yet true; as unknown, and yet well known; as dying, and, behold, we live ; as chastened, and not killed ; as sorrowful, yet always rejoicing ; as poor, yet making many rich ; as having nothing, and yet possessing all things. [*2 Cor. vi.*]

Surely he hath borne our griefs, and carried our sorrows ; yet we did esteem him stricken, smitten of God, and afflicted. But he was wounded for our transgressions, he was bruised for our iniquities : the chastisement of our peace was upon him ; and with his stripes we are healed. [*Isa. liii.*]

Be patient therefore, brethren, unto the coming of the Lord. Behold, the husbandman waiteth for the precious fruit of the earth, and hath long patience for it, until he receive the early and latter rain. Be ye also patient, stablish your hearts : for the coming of the Lord draweth nigh. Murmur not one against another, brethren, lest ye be condemned : behold, the judge standeth before the door. Take, my brethren, the prophets, who have spoken in the name of the Lord, for an example of suffering, affliction, and patience. Behold, we count them happy which endure. Ye have heard of the patience of Job, and have seen the end of the Lord ; that the Lord is very pitiful, and of tender mercy. [*Jas. v.*] For God is not unrighteous to forget your work and labor of love, which ye have shewed toward his name, in that ye have ministered to the saints, and do minister. And we desire that every one of you do shew the same diligence to the full assurance of hope unto the end : that ye be not slothful, but followers of them who through faith and patience inherit the promises. [*Heb. vi.*] Better is the end of a thing than the beginning thereof: and the patient in spirit is better than the proud in spirit. [*Eccl. vii.*]

Wherefore, seeing we also are compassed about with so great a cloud of witnesses, let us lay aside every weight, and the sin which doth so easily beset us, and let us run with patience the race that is set before us, looking unto Jesus the author and finisher of our faith; who for the joy that was set before him endured the cross, despising the shame, and is set down at the right hand of the throne of God. For consider him that endured such contradiction of sinners against himself, lest ye be wearied and faint in your minds. Ye have not yet resisted unto blood, striving against sin. [*Heb. xii.*]

Now the God of patience and consolation grant you to be likeminded one toward another according to Christ Jesus: that ye may with one mind and one mouth glorify God, even the Father of our Lord Jesus Christ. [*Rom. xv.*]

GENTLENESS AND LOVE.

When he giveth quietness, who then can make trouble? [*Job xxxiv.*] For thus saith the Lord God, the Holy One of Israel; In returning and rest shall ye be saved; in quietness and in confidence shall be your strength. [*Isa. xxx.*] And the work of righteousness shall be peace; and the effect of righteousness, quietness and assurance for ever. And my people shall dwell in a peaceable habitation, and in sure dwellings, and in quiet resting places. [*Isa. xxxii.*] But let it be the hidden man of the heart, in that which is not corruptible, even the ornament of a meek and quiet spirit, which is in the sight of God of great price. [*1 Peter iii.*]

Who is a wise man and endued with knowledge among you? let him shew out of a good conversation his works with meekness of wisdom. But if ye have bitter envying and strife in your hearts, glory not, and lie not against the truth. This wisdom descendeth not from above, but is earthly, sensual, devilish. For where envying and strife is, there is confusion and every evil work. But the wisdom that is from above is first pure, then peaceable, gentle, and easy to be entreated, full of mercy and good fruits, without partiality, and without hypocrisy. And the fruit of righteousness is sown in peace for them that make peace. [*Jas. iii.*]

Herein is my Father glorified, that ye bear much fruit; so shall ye be my disciples. As the Father hath loved me, so have I loved you: continue ye in my love. If ye keep my commandments, ye shall abide in my love; even as I have kept my Father's commandments, and abide in his love. These things have I spoken unto you, that my joy might remain in you, and that your joy might be full. This is my commandment, that ye love one another, as I have loved you. Greater love hath no man than this, that a man lay down his life for his friends. Ye are my friends, if ye do whatsoever I command you. Henceforth I call you not servants; for the servant knoweth not what his lord doeth: but I have called you friends. [*John xv.*]

And we have known and believed the love that God

hath to us. God is love; and he that dwelleth in love dwelleth in God, and God in him. Herein is our love made perfect, that we may have boldness in the day of judgment: because as he is, so are we in this world. There is no fear in love; but perfect love casteth out fear: because fear hath torment. He that feareth is not made perfect in love. We love him, because he first loved us. If a man say, I love God, and hateth his brother, he is a liar: for he that loveth not his brother whom he hath seen, how can he love God whom he hath not seen? And this commandment have we from him, that he who loveth God love his brother also. [*1 John iv.*]

He that findeth his life shall lose it: and he that loseth his life for my sake shall find it. He that receiveth you receiveth me; and he that receiveth me receiveth him that sent me. He that receiveth a prophet in the name of a prophet shall receive a prophet's reward; and he that receiveth a righteous man in the name of a righteous man shall receive a righteous man's reward. And whosoever shall give to drink unto one of these little ones a cup of cold water only in the name of a disciple, verily I say unto you, he shall in no wise lose his reward. [*Matt. x.*]

Though I speak with the tongues of men and of angels, and have not charity, I am become as sounding brass, or a tinkling cymbal. And though I have the gift of prophecy, and understand all mysteries, and all knowledge; and though I have all faith, so that I could remove mountains, and have not charity, I am nothing. And though I bestow all my goods to feed the

poor, and though I give my body to be burned, and
have not charity, it profiteth me nothing. Charity suf-
fereth long, and is kind; charity envieth not; charity
vaunteth not itself, is not puffed up, doth not behave
itself unseemly, seeketh not her own, is not easily pro-
voked, thinketh no evil; rejoiceth not in iniquity, but
rejoiceth in the truth; beareth all things, believeth all
things, hopeth all things, endureth all things. Charity
never faileth; but whether there be prophecies, they
shall fail; whether there be tongues, they shall cease;
whether there be knowledge, it shall vanish away. And
now abideth faith, hope, charity, these three; but the
greatest of these is charity. [*1 Cor. xiii.*]

Therefore all things whatsoever ye would that men
should do to you, do ye even so to them: for this is the
law and the prophets. [*Matt. vii.*]   There is that maketh himself rich, yet hath nothing: there is that maketh
himself poor, yet hath great riches. [*Prov. xiii.*]   He
that oppresseth the poor reproacheth his Maker: but
he that honoreth him hath mercy on the poor.   He
that despiseth his neighbor sinneth: but he that hath
mercy on the poor, happy is he. [*Prov. xiv.*]   Is not
this the fast that I have chosen? to loose the bands of
wickedness, to undo the heavy burdens, and to let the
oppressed go free, and that ye break every yoke? Is it
not to deal thy bread to the hungry, and that thou bring
the poor that are cast out to thy house? when thou seest
the naked, that thou cover him; and that thou hide not
thyself from thine own flesh? [*Isa. lviii.*]

And Jesus sat over against the treasury, and beheld

how the people cast money into the treasury: and many that were rich cast in much. And there came a certain poor widow, and she threw in two mites, which make a farthing. And he called unto him his disciples, and saith unto them, Verily I say unto you, that this poor widow hath cast more in, than all they which have cast into the treasury: for all they did cast in of their abundance; but she of her want did cast in all that she had, even all her living. [*Mark xii.*]

Then shall the King say, Come, ye blessed of my Father, inherit the kingdom prepared for you from the foundation of the world: for I was a hungered, and ye gave me meat: I was thirsty, and ye gave me drink: I was a stranger, and ye took me in: naked, and ye clothed me: I was sick, and ye visited me: I was in prison, and ye came unto me. Then shall the righteous answer him, saying, Lord, when saw we thee a hungered, and fed thee? or thirsty, and gave thee drink?

And the King shall answer and say unto them, Verily I say unto you, Inasmuch as ye have done it unto one of the least of these my brethren, ye have done it unto me. [*Matt. xxv.*]

FRIENDSHIP.

Change not a friend for any good by no means; neither a faithful brother for the gold of Ophir. Forego not a wise and good woman: for her grace is above gold. [*Ecclus. vii.*]

And Ruth said, Entreat me not to leave thee, or to

return from following after thee: for whither thou goest, I will go: and where thou lodgest, I will lodge: thy people shall be my people, and thy God my God: where thou diest, will I die, and there will I be buried: the Lord do so to me, and more also, if aught but death part thee and me. [*Ruth i.*]

And it came to pass, that the soul of Jonathan was knit with the soul of David, and Jonathan loved him as his own soul. Then Jonathan and David made a covenant, because he loved him as his own soul. And Jonathan stripped himself of the robe that was upon him, and gave it to David, and his garments, even to his sword, and to his bow, and to his girdle. [*1 Sam. xviii.*)

And David lamented with this lamentation over Saul and over Jonathan his son: The beauty of Israel is slain upon thy high places: how are the mighty fallen! Ye mountains of Gilboa, let there be no dew, neither let there be rain, upon you, nor fields of offerings: for there the shield of the mighty is vilely cast away, the shield of Saul, as though he had not been anointed with oil. From the blood of the slain, from the fat of the mighty, the bow of Jonathan turned not back, and the sword of Saul returned not empty. Saul and Jonathan were lovely and pleasant in their lives, and in their death they were not divided; they were swifter than eagles, they were stronger than lions. Ye daughters of Israel, weep over Saul. How are the mighty fallen in the midst of battle! O Jonathan, thou wast slain in thine high places. I am distressed for thee, my brother Jonathan: very pleasant hast thou been unto me: thy love to me was wonderful, passing the love of women. How are the mighty fallen, and the weapons of war perished! [*2 Sam. i.*]

PURITY AND HUMILITY.

Blessed are the pure in heart: for they shall see God. [*Matt. v.*] He that loveth pureness of heart, for the grace of his lips the king shall be his friend. [*Prov. xxii.*] Pure religion and undefiled before our God and Father is this, to visit the fatherless and widows in their affliction, and to keep himself unspotted from the world. [*Jas. i.*]

Though the Lord be high, yet hath he respect unto the lowly: but the proud he knoweth afar off. [*Ps. cxxxviii.*] He hath shewed strength with his arm; he hath scattered the proud in the imagination of their hearts. He hath put down the mighty from their seats, and exalted them of low degree. [*Luke i.*] The fear of the Lord is the instruction of wisdom; and before honor is humility. [*Prov. xv.*] By humility and the fear of the Lord are riches and honor and life. [*Prov. xxii.*]

And he spake this parable unto certain which trusted in themselves that they were righteous, and despised others: Two men went up into the temple to pray; the one a Pharisee, and the other a publican. The Pharisee stood and prayed thus with himself, God, I thank thee that I am not as other men are, extortioners, unjust, adulterers, or even as this publican. I fast twice in the week, I give tithes of all that I possess. And the publican, standing afar off, would not lift up so much as his

eyes unto heaven, but smote upon his breast, saying, God
be merciful to me a sinner. I tell you, this man went
down to his house justified rather than the other: for
every one that exalteth himself shall be abased; and he
that humbleth himself shall be exalted. [*Luke xviii.*]

Take heed that ye do not your alms before men, to be
seen of them: otherwise ye have no reward of your
Father which is in heaven. Therefore when thou doest
thine alms, do not sound a trumpet before thee, as the
hypocrites do in the synagogues and in the streets, that
they may have glory of men. Verily I say unto you.
They have their reward. But when thou doest alms, let
not thy left hand know what thy right hand doeth.
[*Matt. vi.*] And when thou prayest, thou shalt not be
as the hypocrites are: for they love to pray standing in
the synagogues and in the corners of the streets, that
they may be seen of men. Verily I say unto you, They
have their reward. But thou, when thou prayest, enter
into thy closet, and when thou hast shut thy door, pray
to thy Father which is in secret; and thy Father which
seeth in secret shall reward thee openly. But when ye
pray, use not vain repetitions, as the heathen do: for
they think that they shall be heard for their much speaking. Be not ye therefore like unto them: for your
Father knoweth what things ye have need of, before ye
ask him. [*Matt. vi.*] But the hour cometh, and now
is, when the true worshippers shall worship the Father
in spirit and in truth: for the Father seeketh such to
worship him. God is a Spirit, and they that worship
him must worship him in spirit and in truth. [*John iv.*]

JOY AND FAITH.

And seeing the multitudes, Jesus went up into a mountain: and when he was set, his disciples came unto him: and he opened his mouth, and taught them, saying, Blessed are the poor in spirit: for theirs is the kingdom of heaven. Blessed are they that mourn: for they shall be comforted. Blessed are the meek: for they shall inherit the earth. Blessed are they which do hunger and thirst after righteousness: for they shall be filled. Blessed are the merciful: for they shall obtain mercy. Blessed are the pure in heart; for they shall see God. Blessed are the peacemakers: for they shall be called the children of God. Blessed are they which are persecuted for righteousness' sake: for theirs is the kingdom of heaven. Blessed are ye, when men shall revile you, and persecute you, and shall say all manner of evil against you falsely, for my sake. Rejoice, and be exceeding glad: for great is your reward in heaven: for so persecuted they the prophets which were before you. [*Matt. v.*]

Now therefore hearken unto me, O ye children: for blessed are they that keep my ways. Hear instruction, and be wise, and refuse it not. Blessed is the man that heareth me, watching daily at my gates, waiting at the posts of my doors. For whoso findeth me findeth life, and shall obtain favor of the Lord. But he that sinneth against me wrongeth his own soul: all they that hate me love death. [*Prov. viii.*] Happy is the man that findeth wisdom, and the man that getteth understanding: for the merchandise of it is better than the merchandise of silver, and the gain thereof than fine gold.   She is more precious than rubies: and all the things thou canst desire are not to be compared unto her.   Length of days is in her right hand; and in her left hand riches and honor. Her ways are ways of pleasantness, and all her paths are peace.   She is a tree of life to them that lay hold upon her: and happy is every one that retaineth her. [*Prov. iii.*]

Trust in the Lord with all thine heart; and lean not unto thine own understanding.   In all thy ways acknowledge him, and he shall direct thy paths. [*Prov. iii.*]   Blessed is the man that trusteth in the Lord, and whose hope the Lord is.   For he shall be as a tree planted by the waters, and that spreadeth out her roots by the river, and shall not see when heat cometh, but her leaf shall be green; and shall not be careful in the year of drought, neither shall cease from yielding fruit. [*Jer. xvii.*]   Commit thy works unto the Lord, and thy thoughts shall be established. (*Prov. xvi.*)

Lay not up for yourselves treasures upon earth, where moth and rust doth corrupt, and where thieves break through and steal: but lay up for yourselves treasures in heaven, where neither moth nor rust doth corrupt, and where thieves do not break through nor steal: for where your treasure is, there will your heart be also. [*Matt. vi.*]

Love not the world, neither the things that are in the world.   If any man love the world, the love of the Father is not in him.   For all that is in the world, the lust of the flesh, and the lust of the eyes, and the pride of life, is not of the Father, but is of the world. And the world passeth away, and the lust thereof; but he that doeth the will of God abideth for ever. [*1 John ii.*] Seek ye first the kingdom of God, and his righteousness; and all these things shall be added unto you. Take therefore no thought for the morrow: for the morrow shall take thought for the things of itself. Sufficient unto the day is the evil thereof. [*Matt. vi.*] These things I have spoken unto you, that in me ye might have peace. In the world ye shall have tribulation: but be of good cheer; I have overcome the world. [*John xvi.*]

The hope of the ungodly is like dust that is blown away with the wind; like a thin froth that is driven away with the storm; like as the smoke which is dispersed here and there with a tempest, and passeth away as the remembrance of a guest that tarrieth but a day. But the righteous live for evermore; their reward also is with the Lord, and the care of them is with the Most High. Therefore shall they receive a glorious kingdom, and a beautiful crown from the Lord's hand; for with his right hand shall he cover them, and with his arm shall he protect them. [*Wisdom v.*]

CHILDREN.

At the same time came the disciples unto Jesus, saying, Who is the greatest in the kingdom of heaven? And Jesus called a little child unto him, and set him in the midst of them, and said, Verily I say unto you, except ye be converted, and become as little children, ye shall not enter into the kingdom of heaven. Whosoever therefore shall humble himself as this little child, the same is greatest in the kingdom of heaven. And whoso shall receive one such little child in my name receiveth me. But whoso shall cause one of these little ones which believe in me to stumble, it were better for him that a millstone were hanged about his neck, and that he were drowned in the depth of the sea. Take heed that ye despise not one of these little ones; for I say unto you, that in heaven their angels do always behold the face of my Father which is in heaven. Even so it is not the will of your Father which is in heaven, that one of these little ones should perish. [*Matt. xviii.*] They shall be mine, saith the Lord of hosts, in that day when I make up my jewels; and I will spare them, as a man spareth his own son that serveth him. [*Mal. iii.*]

And they brought young children to him, that he should touch them; and his disciples rebuked those that brought them. But when Jesus saw it, he was much displeased, and said unto them, Suffer the little children to come unto me, and forbid them not; for of such is the kingdom of God. Verily I say unto you, Whosoever shall not receive the kingdom of God as a little child, he shall not enter therein. And he took them up in his arms, put his hands upon them, and blessed them. [*Mark x.*]

A voice was heard in Ramah, lamentation, and bitter weeping; Rachel weeping for her children refused to be comforted for her children, because they were not. Thus saith the Lord; Refrain thy voice from weeping, and thine eyes from tears : (for thy work shall be rewarded,) saith the Lord. [*Jer. xxxi.*]

When David saw that his servants whispered, David perceived that the child was dead : therefore David said unto his servants, Is the child dead? And they said, He is dead. Then David arose from the earth, and washed, and anointed himself, and changed his apparel, and came into the house of the Lord, and worshipped : then he came to his own house ; and when he required, they set bread before him, and he did eat. Then said his servants unto him, What thing is this that thou hast done? thou didst fast and weep for the child, while it was alive ; but when the child was dead, thou didst arise and eat bread. And he said, While the child was yet alive, I fasted and wept : for I said, Who can tell whether God will be gracious to me, that the child may live? But now he is dead, wherefore should I fast? can I bring him back again? I shall go to him, but he shall not return to me. [*2 Sam. xii.*]

And it came to pass, when the man of God saw the woman afar off, that he said to his servant : Run now, I pray thee, to meet her, and say unto her, Is it well with thee? is it well with thy husband? is it well with the child? And she answered, It is well. [*2 Kings iv.*]

And David was much moved, and went up to the chamber over the gate, and wept : and as he went, thus he said, O my son Absalom! my son, my son Absalom! would God I had died for thee, O Absalom, my son, my son! [*2 Sam. xviii.*] And the victory that day was turned into mourning unto all the people : for the people heard say that day how the king was grieved for his son. And the people gat them by stealth that day into the city, as people being ashamed steal away when they flee in battle.   But the king covered his face, and the king cried with a loud voice, O my son Absalom !   O Absalom, my son, my son ! [*2 Sam. xix.*]

MEN AND WOMEN.

Though the righteous be prevented with death, yet shall he be in rest.   For honorable age is not that which standeth in length of time, nor that is measured by number of years.   But wisdom is the gray hair unto men, and an unspotted life is old age.   He pleased God, and was beloved of him : so that living among sinners he was translated.   He, being made perfect in a short time, fulfilled a long time : for his soul pleased the Lord : (therefore hasted he to take him away from among the wicked)   This the people saw, and understood it not, neither laid they up this in their minds, that his grace and mercy is with his saints, and that he hath respect unto his chosen.   Thus the righteous that is dead shall condemn the ungodly which are living : and youth that is soon perfected the many years and old age of the unrighteous. [*Wisdom iv.*]

Leave thy fatherless children, I will preserve them alive ; and let thy widows trust in me. [*Jer. xlix.*] Come, ye children, hearken unto me : I will teach you the fear of the Lord.   What man is he that desireth life, and loveth many days, that he may see good?   Keep thy tongue from evil, and thy lips from speaking guile. Depart from evil, and do good; seek peace, and pursue it. [*Ps. xxxiv.*] Honor thy father with thy whole heart, and forget not the sorrows of thy mother. Remember that thou wast begotten of them; and how canst thou recompense them the things that they have done for thee? [*Ecclus. vii.*] My son, keep thy father's commandment, and forsake not the law of thy mother: bind them continually upon thine heart, and tie them about thy neck. When thou goest, it shall lead thee; when thou sleepest, it shall keep thee; and when thou awakest, it shall talk with thee. For the commandment is a lamp; and the law is light; and reproofs of instruction are the way of life. [*Prov. vi.*] counsel: O how comely is the wisdom of old men, and understanding and counsel to men of honor! Much experience is the crown of old men, and the fear of God is their glory. [*Ecclus. xxv.*]

The hoary head is a crown of glory, if it be found in the way of righteousness. He that is slow to anger is better than the mighty; and he that ruleth his spirit than he that taketh a city. The lot is cast into the lap; but the whole disposing thereof is of the Lord. [*Prov. xvi.*] Then Abraham gave up the ghost, and died in a good old age, an old man, and full of years; and was gathered to his people. [*Gen. xxv.*] And he died in a good old age, full of days, riches, and honor. [*I Chro. xxix.*]

O God thou hast taught me from my youth: and hitherto have I declared thy wondrous works. Now also when I am old and grayheaded, O God, forsake me not. Cast me not off in the time of old age; forsake me not when my strength faileth. [*Ps. lxxi.*]

If thou prepare thine heart, and stretch out thine hands toward him; if iniquity be in thine hand, put it far away, and let not wickedness dwell in thy tabernacles. For then shalt thou lift up thy face without spot; yea, thou shalt be steadfast, and shalt not fear: because thou shalt forget thy misery, and remember it as waters that pass away: and thine age shall be clearer than the noonday; thou shalt shine forth, and shalt be as the morning. And thou shalt be secure, because there is hope; yea, thou shalt dig about thee, and thou shalt take thy rest in safety. [*Job xi.*] And thou shalt go to thy fathers in peace; thou shalt be buried in a good old age. [*Gen xv.*] Thou shalt come to thy grave in a full age, like as a shock of corn cometh in his season. [*Job. v.*]

The righteous shall flourish like the palm tree: he shall grow like a cedar in Lebanon. Those that be planted in the house of the Lord shall flourish in the courts of our God. They shall still bring forth fruit in old age; to shew that the Lord is upright: he is my rock, and there is no unrighteousness in him. [*Ps. xcii.*] Hearken unto me, O house of Jacob, and all the remnant of the house of Israel. Even to your old age I am he: and even to hoar hairs will I carry you; I have made, and I will bear; even I will carry, and will deliver you. [*Isa. xlvi.*] Return unto thy rest, O my soul; for the Lord hath dealt bountifully with thee. For thou hast delivered my soul from death, mine eyes from tears, and my feet from falling. [*Ps. cxvi.*]

Remember now thy Creator in the days of thy youth,

first heaven and the first earth were passed away; and there was no more sea. And I John saw the holy city, new Jerusalem, coming down from God out of heaven. And I heard a great voice out of heaven saying, Behold, the tabernacle of God is with men, and he will dwell with them, and they shall be his people, and God himself shall be with them, and be their God. And God shall wipe away all tears from their eyes; and there shall be no more death, neither sorrow, nor crying, neither shall there be any more pain: for the former things are passed away. And he that sat upon the throne said, Behold, I make all things new. I am Alpha and Omega, the beginning and the end. I will give unto him that is athirst of the fountain of the water of life freely. He that overcometh shall inherit all things; and I will be his God, and he shall be my son. [*Rev. xxi.*] And I heard a voice from heaven saying unto me, Write, Blessed are the dead which die in the Lord from henceforth: yea, saith the Spirit, that they may rest from their labors; and their works do follow them. [*Rev. xiv.*] They shall not hunger nor thirst; neither shall the heat nor sun smite them: for he that hath mercy on them shall lead them, even by the springs of water shall he guide them. [*Isa. xlix.*]

And he shewed me a pure river of water of life, clear as crystal. On either side of the river, was there the tree of life, and the leaves of the tree were for the healing of the nations. And there shall be no night there; and they need no candle, neither light of the sun; for the Lord God giveth them light: and they shall reign for ever and ever. [*Rev. xxii.*] And the city hath no need of the sun, neither of the moon, to shine in it; for the glory of God did lighten it, and the Lamb is the light thereof. [And the nations shall walk in the light of it: and the kings of the earth do bring their glory and honor into it.] And the gates of it shall not be shut at all by day: for there shall be no night there. [*Rev. xxi.*]

Strengthen ye the weak hands, and confirm the feeble knees. Say to them that are of a fearful heart, Be strong, fear not: behold, your God will come with vengeance, even God with a recompense; he will come and save you. Then the eyes of the blind shall be opened, and the ears of the deaf shall be unstopped. Then shall the lame man leap as a hart, and the tongue of the dumb sing: for in the wilderness shall waters break out, and streams in the desert. And the parched ground shall become a pool, and the thirsty land springs of water. And a highway shall be there, and a way, and it shall be called The way of holiness; the unclean shall not pass over it; but it shall be for those: the wayfaring men, though fools, shall not err therein. And the ransomed of the Lord shall return, and come to Zion with songs and everlasting joy upon their heads: they shall obtain joy and gladness, and sorrow and sighing shall flee away. [*Isa. xxxv.*]

After this I beheld, and, lo, a great multitude, which no man could number, of all nations, and kindreds, and people, and tongues, stood before the throne, and before the Lamb, clothed with white robes, and palms in their hands: and cried with a loud voice, saying, Salvation to

our God which sitteth upon the throne, and unto the
Lamb. And all the angels stood round about the throne,
and worshipped God, saying, Amen : Blessing, and glory,
and wisdom, and thanksgiving, and honor, and power,
and might, be unto our God for ever and ever. Amen.
Who are these which are arrayed in white robes, and
whence came they? These are they which came out of
great tribulation, and have washed their robes, and
made them white in the blood of the Lamb. Therefore
are they before the throne of God, and serve him day and
night in his temple : and he that sitteth on the throne
shall dwell among them. They shall hunger no more,
neither thirst any more; neither shall the sun light on
them, nor any heat. For the Lamb which is in the
midst of the throne shall feed them, and shall lead them
unto living fountains of waters : and God shall wipe
away all tears from their eyes. [*Rev. vii.*]

Now the God of hope fill you with all joy and peace,
that ye may abound in hope, through the power of the
Holy Spirit. [*Rom. xv.*]

THOUGHTS OF IMMORTALITY

The soul lives after the body dies. The soul passes through the gate; he makes a way in the darkness to his Father; he has pierced the heart of evil to do the things of his Father.

Then shall the Judge of the dead answer: Let this soul pass on; he is without sin; he lives upon truth. He has made his delight in doing what is good to men, and what is pleasing to God. He has given food to the hungry; drink to the thirsty and clothes to the naked. His lips are pure and his hands are pure. His heart weighs right in the balance. He fought on earth the battle of the good, even as his Father, the Lord of the invisible world had commanded him. O God, the protector of him who has brought his cry unto Thee, make it well with him in the world of spirits! He loved his father, he honored his mother; he loved his brethren. He never preferred the great man to him of low condition. He was a wise man, his soul loved God. He was a brother to the great and a father to the humble; and he never was a mischief-maker. Such as these shall find grace in the eyes of the great God. They shall dwell in the abodes of glory, where the heavenly life is led. The bodies which they have abandoned will repose forever in their tombs, while they will enjoy the presence of the great God. — *Egyptian* (*Book of the Dead*).

(80)

Heaven is a palace with many doors, and each one may enter in his own way.   There is another, invisible, eternal existence, superior to the visible one, which does not perish when all things perish.   Those who attain to this never return.   The God of the dead waits enthroned in immortal light to welcome the good into his kingdom of joy ; to the homes he has prepared for them, where the One Being dwells beyond the stars. — *Hindu.*

There are treasures laid up in the heart— treasures of charity, piety, temperance, and soberness.   These treasures a man takes with him beyond death, when he leaves this world.   Man never dies.   The soul inhabits the body for a time and leaves it again.   The soul is myself ; the body is only my dwelling-place.   The pearls and gems which a man has collected, even from his youth, cannot go with him to another world.   Friends and relations cannot go with him a step further than his place of burial.   But a man's actions, good or bad, go with him to the future world.   As kindred, friends and dear ones salute him who hath travelled far and returned home safe, so will good deeds welcome him who goes from this world and enters another. — *Buddhist.*

What is death? To be born again an angel of Eternity. — *Persian (Buzurdi).*
The Supreme Soul, whose work is the universe, always dwelling in the hearts of all being, is revealed by the heart.   Those who know him become immortal. — *Hindu.*
The sun rises out of life and sets into life ; this is the sacred law ; it sways to-day, and will sway to-morrow.

From the unreal, lead me to the real; from darkness to light; from death to immortality! This uttered overcomes the world. — *Hindu* (*Brihad Upanishad*).

Know that these finite bodies have belonged to an eternal, inexhaustible, indestructible spirit. He who believes that this spirit can kill, and he who believes it can be killed, both are wrong. Unborn, changeless, eternal, it is not slain when the body is slain. * * * * Weapons cannot cleave, nor fire burn it. It is constant, immovable; yet it can pass through all things. * * * * Grieve not then for any creatures, and abandon not thy duty. For a noble man, that infamy were worse than death. * * * * It is good to die doing thy own work. —*Hindu* (*Bhagavadgitá*).

Virtue is a service man owes himself; and though there were no heaven, nor any God to rule the world, it were not less the binding law of life. It is a man's privilege to know the right and follow it.

Betray and persecute me, brother men! * * * * Earth, hell, heaven, combine your might to crush, — I will still hold fast by this inheritance! My strength is nothing — time can shake and cripple it; my youth is transient — already grief has withered up my days; my heart — alas! it seems well nigh broken now! Anguish may crush it utterly, and life may fail; but even so my soul, that has not tripped, shall triumph, and dying, give the lie to soulless Destiny, that dares to boast itself man's master. — *Hindu* (*Rámáyana*).

Man must not be carried away by grief, but hasten to

a better mind. Thou hast shed tears: it is enough.
* * * * We have given what we ought to grief; now
let us do what is becoming. — *Hindu* (*Râmâyana*).

Why lookest thou so dull upon thy friends, thou to
whom thy friends were so dear? Thy face seems to
smile on us in the bosom of death, as if thou wert alive.
We see thy glory still, like sunset on a mountain's head.
— *Hindu*.

He who in the morning has seen the right way, may
in the evening die without regret. — *Confucius*.

It is right, my friends, that we should consider this:
that if the soul is immortal, it requires our care not only
for the present time, which we call life, but for all time.
He, then, is truly wise, who considers most about his
soul; who having adorned his soul, not with a foreign,
but with its own proper ornament, — temperance, justice,
fortitude, freedom, and truth, — thus waits for his passage
to the world of the departed, as one who is ready to go
whenever destiny shall summon him.

If death be the journey to another place, and there all
the dead are, what good can be greater than this? Be
of good cheer about death, and know this of a truth, —
that no evil can happen to a good man, either in life or
after death. — *Plato*.

The body is a prison, from which the soul must be
released before it can arrive at the knowledge of things
real and immutable.

The soul of each of us is an immortal spirit, and goes
to other immortals to give an account of its actions.

When thou shalt have laid aside thy body, thou shalt

rise, freed from mortality, and become an inhabitant of the kindly skies.

My body must descend to the place ordained, but my soul will not descend: being a thing immortal, it will ascend on high, where it will enter a heavenly abode. Death does not differ at all from life.

Every soul is immortal; for whatever is continually moved is immortal. Every body which is moved from without is soulless, but that which is moved from within, that is, of itself, possesses a soul, since this is the very nature of soul. But if this be the case, — that there is nothing else which moves itself except soul, — soul must necessarily be (both uncreate and) immortal. — *Plato.*

> All that God works is effortless and calm:
>   Seated on loftiest throne,
>   Thence, though we know not how,
>   He works his perfect will.
>   — *Æschylus (The Suppliants).*

> It is shame
> For any man to wish for length of life,
> Who, wrapt in troubles, knows no change for good.
> For what delight brings day still following day,
> Or bringing on, or putting off our death?
> I would not rate that man as worth regard
> Whose fervor glows on vain and empty hopes:
> But either noble life or noble death
> Becomes the gently born. — *Sophocles (Ajax).*

An immortal man established in righteousness is a noble hymn of God. — *Greek.*

Who knows whether to live is not death, and to die, life? — *Euripides.*

I believe Nature, knowing the confusion and shortness of our life, hath industriously concealed the end of it from us, this making for our advantage; for if we were sensible of it beforehand, some would pine away with untimely sorrow, and would die before their death came.

Every one should meditate seriously with himself, that it is not the longest life which is the best, but that which is the most virtuous.

But such exclamations as this, " The young man ought not to be taken off so abruptly in the vigor of his years," are very frivolous, and proceed from a great weakness of mind; for who is it that can say what a thing ought to be?

And who knows but that the Deity, with a fatherly providence and out of tenderness to mankind, foreseeing what would happen, hath taken some purposely out of this life by an untimely death? So we should think that nothing has befallen them which they should have sought to shun, — " For naught that cometh by necessity is hard." — *Plutarch.*

What then do you wish to be doing when you are found by death? I, for my part, would wish to be found doing something which belongs to a man, beneficent, suitable to the general interest, noble. But if I cannot be found doing things so great, I would be found doing at least that which I cannot be hindered from doing, that which is permitted me to do : correcting myself, laboring at tranquillity of mind, rendering to the relations of life their due.

If death surprises me when I am busy about these things, it is enough for me if I can stretch out my hands to God and say: The means which I have received from thee for seeing thy administration of the world, and following it, I have not neglected; I have not dishonored thee by my acts. * * * * That thou hast given me life, I thank thee for what thou hast given : so long as I have used the things which are thine I am content ; take them back and place them wherever thou mayest choose ; for thine were all things, thou gavest them to me.

I think that what God chooses is better than what I choose ; I will attach myself as minister and follower to him. — *Epictetus.*

When I consider the faculties with which the human soul is endowed, * * * * I feel a conscious conviction that this active, comprehensive principle cannot possibly be of a mortal nature. And as this unceasing activity of the soul derives its energy from its own intrinsic and essential powers, without receiving it from any foreign or external impulse, it necessarily follows that its activity must continue forever.

I consider this world as a place which Nature never intended for my permanent abode ; and I look on my departure from it, not as being driven from my habitation, but simply as leaving an inn. — *Cicero.*

That which we call death is but a pause or suspension, and in truth a progress to life : only our thoughts look downward upon the body, and not forward upon things to come. It is the care of a wise and good man to look to his manners and actions ; and rather how well he lives than how long. To die sooner or later is not the business, but to die well or ill ; for death brings us to immortality.

Why was such a one taken away in the prime of his years? Life is to be measured by action, not by time. A man may die old at thirty, and young at fourscore. Nay, the one lives after death; and the other perished before he died. The fear of death is a continual slavery, as the contempt of it is certain liberty. — *Seneca.*

Day and night show unto us the resurrection. The night falleth asleep and the day ariseth; the day departeth and night cometh on. Let us mark how and in what manner the sowing taketh place. The sower casteth into the earth each of the seeds and these decay: then out of their decay the might of the Master's providence raiseth them up and they bear fruit. — *Clement of Rome.*

Vines hold not their clusters all the year; now are they fruitful, and now they shed their leaves like tears. Like the sun, the pure are clouded. On them the envious crowd may hurl its hate; but it is as sparks falling on the clear stream — the sparks perish, the water goes shining on. Fear not the dark, friend; perchance the Water of Life may be found in the dark abyss of sorrow. — *Persian (Saadi).*

We saw him in the garden, the pleasant garden,
With his companions and his children, the children he loved.
His children and his servants blessed him.
His home was the shelter of happiness.
    Peace be upon him.
We saw him giving food to the hungry,
And clothing to the naked.
We saw him give help and succor to the aged,
And good counsel to the young.

He suffered not the stranger to sleep in the streets:
He opened his door to the wayfarer.
        Peace be upon him. — *Syrian Dirge.*

Yes, the very least and the very greatest sorrows that
God ever suffers to befall thee, proceed from the depths
of his unspeakable love; and such great love were better
for thee than the highest and best gifts besides that he
has given thee, or ever could give thee, if thou could'st
but see it in this light.

God is ever ready, but we are very unready; God
is nigh to us, but we are far from him; God is within,
we are without; God is at home, we are strangers.
The prophet says: "God leadeth the righteous by a
narrow path into a broad highway, till they come
into a wide and open place": that is, unto the true
freedom of that spirit which hath become one spirit with
God. God help us all to follow him, that he may
bring us unto himself! — *John Tauler.*

Lord, I know not what I ought to ask of thee; thou
lovest me better than I can love myself. O my Father,
give to thy child that which he knows not how to ask.
I dare not pray either for crosses or consolations; I
present myself before thee, I open my heart to thee.
Behold those wants that I know not myself. See and do
according to thy tender mercy.

I adore thy will without knowing it. I am silent
before thee; I yield myself up, I would sacrifice myself
to thy will, I could have no other desire than to do it.
Teach me to pray; pray thyself in me.

O my God! what is death or life to me? Life is
nothing; it is even a snare if it be too dear to me.

Death can only destroy this house of clay; it delivers the soul from the contamination of the body, and from its own pride. It frees it from the influence of the tempter, and introduces it forever into the kingdom of truth.

I ask not, then, O my Father, for health or for life. I make an offering to thee of all my days. Thou hast counted them. I would know nothing more. All I ask is to die rather than live as I have lived, and if it be thy will that I depart, let me die in patience and in love. Almighty God, who holdest the keys of the tomb in thy hand, to open and close it at thy will, give me not life if I love it too well. Living or dying, I would be thine. — *Fenelon.*

All death in nature is birth, and in death appears visibly the advancement of life. There is no killing principle in nature, for nature throughout is life; it is not death which kills, but the higher life, which, concealed behind the other, begins to develop itself. Death and birth are but the struggle of life with itself to attain a higher form. —*J. G. Fichte.*

No set words or thoughts will enable us to meet death trustfully. Such trust is God's gift, and the more we detach ourselves from all save Himself, the more "freely He will give us" this, as all other blessings. Once attain to losing self in God, and death will indeed have no sting. —*Jean Nicolas Grou.*

Wherever I may be, through whatever worlds I may be led, I know that I shall forever remain in the hands of the Father who brought me hither, and calls me further on. — *Herder.*

                    Then woke
Stirrings of deep Divinity within,
And, like the flickerings of a smouldering flame,
Yearnings of a hereafter.   Thou it was,
When the world's din and passion's voice was still,
Calling thy wanderer home. — *Williams*.

   What shall I do to gain eternal life?
        Discharge aright
The simple dues with which each day is rife,
        Yea, with thy might.
Ere perfect scheme of action thou devise,
        Thy life is fled.
But he who ever acts as conscience cries,
        Shall live though dead. — *Schiller*.

He has gone before us.   The spirit within him that
used to talk to us, to look at us with kind eyes, has left
the body, and is no longer visible.   Blessings on his
memory!   May he also, if he behold us, bless us! for
we need his blessing.   Greatly we need it, with these
hopeless yearnings for his presence; these fears that we
did not do all we might have done for him; this almost
shame at feeling that we are warm and living, while he
is cold and motionless; at home and housed, while he
is away.

But these are our thoughts, not his.   His body is not
his spirit; and perhaps his spirit looks upon us this
moment, and sees how we loved him, and how we
suffer.   He knows the struggles that we have still to
endure; he looks on his mortal friends with immortal
kindness; on these dear relations, on these beloved children.   Let us be calm in the hope of rejoining him; let
us become patient in it; let us rejoice in it.   Let us
cherish the thoughts he would desire; let us take up

again the duties he would wish us, now and ever, to perform.

O friends that remain! ye will keep as much of me as ye are able; kind thoughts of me; recollections of our mutual joys and sufferings; recollection of the pardon we gave to each other. You will love all whom I have loved, and me in them.

Surely love, and hope, and joy are not confined to us. Surely there are myriads of beings inhabiting the invisible world. Some may have realized their heaven, and are resting. Some may be carrying it further. Some may be helping us, just as we help the bee, or the wounded bird; spirits of dear friends, who still pity our tears, rejoice in our smiles, and whisper into our hearts a belief that they are present.

The heart bids us believe it possible; and oh! whatever good thing the heart bids us believe, let us do our best to believe it; for God has put it there, and its goodness is His warrant for its being cherished. — *Leigh Hunt.*

The immortality of the soul is a truth which is not bright except to the pure in heart.

Through making us hope for immortality, God has made us a promise of it. If faith is the evidence of things not seen, hope is the certainty of them. Hope prophesies to us. Hope makes us free of the universe. I am a pilgrim, and life is what I have to travel over; and oh! I have many dangers and many wants; but hope is my all in all, nearly. Hope is light, and courage, and a staff; and when I sit down, it is a friend to talk with; and when I suffer, it is an angel to stand by and strengthen me ; and when I have wandered away in sin, and repented and returned to the right path, then from hope I get my peace of mind again, and newness of virtue.

The morrow of the world is a purpose in the mind of God, and so is the great to-morrow of my soul. And I can be well contented to have my life subside on the bosom of him in whom the day died away this evening so beautifully, and in whom it will begin again in the morning so grandly.

O, if there is a heaven for our faith, there are friends in it for our love. Love is greater than faith.

There are some great souls, the very thought of whom is an increase of faith.

A truthful heart never breaks ; it strengthens to the last. And to the last we will trust. God is almighty ; then all things are his mightiness, and all life is his will. * * * * And to us joys shall be the will of God, and so shall pains and sorrows be. Providence is in all things, so that whatever we do not understand shall be to us nothing to be frightened about, but it shall be mystery and the will of God.

I know that darkness is good for me, as well as light, and that it is good for me not to know some things, as well as to know others ; and for myself, I can pray to God out of my whole heart, and with the strength of my understanding, " Thy will be done on earth, as it is in heaven " ; else there is not a flower, nor an insect, nor a bird, nor an animal, nor a day, nor a man, but might make me question myself to madness. — *William Mountford.*

Know of a truth that only the Time-shadows have

perished, or are perishable; that the real being of whatever was, and whatever is, and whatever will be, *is* even now and forever.

Can the earth, which is but dead, and a vision, resist Spirits, which have reality, and are alive? On the hardest adamant some footprint of us is stamped in. The last rear of the host will read traces of the earliest van. But whence? O Heaven, whither? Sense knows not; faith knows not; only that it is through mystery into mystery, from God to God. — *Thomas Carlyle.*

Of what import this vacant sky, these puffing elements, these insignificant lives, full of selfish loves, and quarrels, and ennui? Every thing is prospective, and man is to live hereafter. That the world is for his education is the only sane solution of the enigma. All the comfort I have found, teaches me to confide that I shall not have less in times and places that I do not yet know. All I have seen teaches me to trust the Creator for all I have not seen. Whatever it be which the great Providence prepares for us, it must be something large and generous, and in the great style of his works.

The love that will be annihilated sooner than be treacherous has already made death impossible, and affirms itself no mortal, but a native of the deeps of absolute and inextinguishable being. — *R. W. Emerson.*

> 'Tis only when they spring to heaven that angels
> Reveal themselves to you; they sit all day
> Beside you; and lie down at night by you,
> Who care not for their presence — muse or sleep —
> And all at once they leave you and you know them!

Dear Festus, lay me,
When I shall die, within some narrow grave,
Not by itself — for that would be too proud —
But where such graves are thickest: let it look
Nowise distinguished from the hillocks round,
So that the peasant at his brother's bed
May tread upon my own and know it not;
And we shall all be equal at the last,
Or classed according to life's natural ranks,
Fathers, sons, brothers, friends — not rich, nor wise,
Nor gifted.
                    In man's self arise
August anticipations, symbols, types
Of a dim splendor ever on before,
In that eternal circle run by life:
For men begin to pass their nature's bound,
And find new hopes and cares which fast supplant
Their proper joys and griefs; and outgrow all
The narrow creeds of right and wrong, which fade
Before the unmeasured thirst for good; while peace
Rises within them ever more and more.
                    If I stoop
Into a dark, tremendous sea of cloud,
It is but for a time; I press God's lamp
Close to my breast — its splendor, soon or late,
Will pierce the gloom: I shall emerge one day!
                              Robert Browning.

The life of the Spirit is the evidence [of immortality].
Heaven begun is the living proof that makes the heaven
to come credible. "Christ in you is the hope of glory."
It is the eagle eye of faith which penetrates the grave,
and sees far into the tranquil things of death. He alone
can believe in immortality who feels the resurrection in
him already. — *F. W. Robertson.*

We live in deeds, not years; in thoughts, not breath;
In feelings, not in figures on a dial.

We should count time by heart-throbs.
He most lives
Who thinks most, feels the noblest, acts the best.
Life is but a means unto an end; that end,
Beginning, mean and end to all things, God! — *Bailey*.

We have all felt, when looking above us into the atmosphere, that there was an infinity of space which we could not explore. When I look into man's spirit, and see there the germs of an immortal life, I feel more deeply that an infinity lies hid beyond what I see. In the idea of duty, which springs up in every human heart, I discern a law more sacred and boundless than gravitation, which binds the soul to a more glorious universe than that to which attraction binds the body, and which is to endure though the laws of physical nature pass away. Every moral sentiment, every intellectual action, is to me a hint, a prophetic sign, of a spiritual power to be expanded forever, just as a faint ray from a distant star is significant of unimaginable splendor.

Dream not of a heaven into which you may enter, live as you may. To such as waste the present state, the future will not, cannot bring happiness. There is no concord between them and that world of purity. A human being who has lived without God, and without self-improvement, can no more enjoy heaven than a mouldering body, lifted from the tomb and placed amidst beautiful prospects, can enjoy the light through its decayed eyes, or feel the balmy air which blows away its dust.

Heaven is in truth revealed to us in every pure affection of the human heart, and in every wise and beneficent action that uplifts the soul in adoration and gratitude.

For heaven is only purity, wisdom, benevolence, joy, peace, in their perfected form. Thus the immortal life may be said to surround us perpetually. Some beams of its glory shine upon us in whatever is lovely, heroic, and virtuously happy in ourselves or in others. The pure mind carries heaven within itself, and manifests that heaven to all around.

Immortal happiness is nothing more than the unfolding of our own minds, the full, bright exercise of our best powers; and these powers are never to be unfolded here or hereafter, but through our own free exertion.

The truth is that all action on earth, even the intensest, is but the sport of childhood compared with the energy and activity of that higher life. It must be so. For what principles are so active as intellect, benevolence, the love of truth, the thirst for perfection, sympathy with the suffering, and devotion to God's purposes? and these are the ever-expanding principles of the future life. — *W. E. Channing.*

> So live that when thy summons comes to join
> The innumerable caravan, which moves
> To that mysterious realm where each shall take
> His chamber in the silent halls of death,
> Thou go not like the quarry-slave at night,
> Scourged to his dungeon, but sustained and soothed
> By an unfaltering trust, approach thy grave,
> Like one who wraps the drapery of his couch
> About him and lies down to pleasant dreams.— *W. C. Bryant.*

I see the autumn prefigured in the spring. The flowers of May-day foretold the harvest, its rosy apples, and its yellow ears of corn. As the bud now lying cold and close upon the bark of every tree throughout our northern clime is a silent prophecy of yet another spring and other summers, and harvests too, so this instinctive love of justice, scantily budding here and nipped by adverse fate, silently but clearly tells of the kingdom of heaven.

I cannot think the future world is to be feared, even by the worst of men. I had rather die a sinner than live one. Doubtless justice is there to be done; that may seem stern and severe. But remember, God's justice is not like a man's; it is not vengeance, but mercy; not poison, but medicine. To me it seems tuition more than chastisement. God is not the jailer of the universe, but the Shepherd of the people; not the hangman of mankind, but their Physician; yes, our Father. I cannot fear him as I fear man. I cannot fail to love. * * * * * Does not even the hireling shepherd, when a single lamb has gone astray, leave the ninety and nine safe in their fold, go forth some stormy night and seek the wanderer, rejoicing to bring home the lost one on his shoulders? And shall God forget his child, his frailest or most stubborn child; leave him in endless misery, a prey to insatiate sin, — that grim, bloodthirsty wolf, prowling about the human fold? I tell you no; not God.

The more I live, the more I love this lovely world; feel more its Author in each little thing, in all that is great. But yet I feel my immortality the more. In childhood the consciousness of immortal life buds forth feeble, though full of promise. In the man it unfolds its fragrant petals, his most celestial flower, to mature its seed throughout eternity. — *Theodore Parker*.

God judges by a light
Which baffles mortal sight.
In His vast world above,
A world of broader love,
God hath some grand employment for his son. — *Faber*.

More and more do I feel that this nature of mine is the deep ground-warrant for faith in God and immortality. Everywhere in creation there is a proportion between means and ends, — between all natures and their destinies. And can it be that my soul, which, in its few days' unfolding, is already stretching out its hands to God and to eternity, and which has all its being and welfare wrapped up in those sublime verities, is made to strive and sigh for them in vain, to stretch out its hands to — nothing?

"Onward!" is the call of many a great hour of our being; "onward! to the battle — and victory!" And to this earth-strife that presses upon us every day, to this solemn waiting, — to this dim bordering upon the realm of boundless light, is there not a voice that says, "Onward! onward forever!" Beautiful phrase that describes the departed, "they have passed on." Not, "they are dead"; but — "they have passed on"!

Progress, then, is our being's motto and hope. Gaining and losing in this world, rising and falling, enjoying and suffering, are but the incidents of life. Learning, aspiration, progress, is the life of life. Onward! then, pilgrims to eternity! The day is far spent for some of us, the night is at hand; and over its sublime portal through which the evening stars of this world, but the morning stars of eternity, are shining, is written, "Eye hath not seen, nor ear heard, neither have entered into the heart of man, the things which God hath prepared for them that love him."

Death! what art thou to the Christian's assurance? Great hour of answer to life's prayer; great hour that shall break asunder the bond of life's mystery; hour of release from life's burden; hour of reunion with the loved and lost; what mighty hopes hasten to their fulfilment in thee! What longings, what aspirations, breathe in the still night beneath the silent stars; what dread emotions of curiosity; what deep meditations of joy; what hallowed imaginings of never experienced purity and bliss; what possibilities shadowing forth unspeakable realities to the soul, all verge to their consummation in thee! O death! the Christian's death! what art thou but the gate of life, the portal of heaven, the threshold of eternity? — *Orville Dewey.*

> Our birth is but a sleep and a forgetting:
> The soul that riseth with us, our life's star,
>   Hath had elsewhere its setting,
>   And cometh from afar;
>   Not in entire forgetfulness,
>   And not in utter nakedness,
> But trailing clouds of glory do we come
>   From God, who is our home. — *Wordsworth.*

Let us learn to look on death as an appointment, not a fatality; as an appointment of our Heavenly Father, who alone has the power; as appointed in wisdom and love, because appointed by him. * * * * * To die, is to be set free; free from the fetters of a body which is dying while it lives, and from the narrow bounds of a restricted state. To die, is to go with our conscience and character only, into the presence of our Judge. To

every temple there is a portal, and a passage from the one
to the other.   This mortal life is the portal which stands
before the grand temple of eternity; and death is the
passage between them. — *F. W. P. Greenwood.*

The very greatness of that love which makes the hour
of separation dark and painful gives rise to high and
holy duties in doing the work which we think the puri-
fied spirits of our friends would wish to have done.
— *Richard Metcalf.*

That future world, instead of a boundless abyss of
darkness is a region of life and light. * * *   While the
sun is above the horizon, the heavens seem empty, and
the earth alone seems looked on by that shining orb.
But as the sun sinks and the shadows fall across the hills,
one by one the stars are ushered into the sky, a glorious
host, innumerable worlds, showing forth the wisdom and
power of God.   Then we perceive how much, all the
time, has been around us, and how infinitely more vast
and sublime was that which in the brightness of day was
unseen, than what was visible.   So revelation draws
aside from the eye of the spirit the veil between, and we
behold the empty void filled with those whom we called
dead, alive again, — the mortal become immortal; and
the earth itself appears but the threshold of a vast abode,
peopled by the creatures and filled with the light of
the infinite Love. — *Ephraim Peabody.*

Let us trustingly leave these matters — where, indeed,
whether trustingly or not, we must leave them — with
the infinite Love which embraces all our loves, and the

infinite Wisdom which comprehends all our needs; assured that the Father of the house whose mansions are many, and the Father of spirits whose goal is one, will find the right place and connections and nurture for every soul he has caused to be; that in the eternities the thing desired will arrive at last; that seeking and finding are divinely evened. Let us rest in the thought that life must be richer than all our experience, nay, than our fondest dreams. — *F. H. Hedge*.

When, by nobler culture, by purer experience, by breathing the air of a higher duty, vitality at length creeps into the soul, the instincts of immortality will wake within us. The word of hope will speak to us a language no longer strange. We shall feel like the captive bird carried accidentally to its own land, when hearing for the first time the burst of kindred song from its native woods, it beats instinctively the bar of its cage in yearning for the free air.

A single instant of the Divine life, spread over all that is simultaneous, is worth an eternity of ours, which at least begins by taking all things one by one. And in proportion as we emerge from this childhood of the mind, and claim our approach to union with God, will the contents of our experience enrich themselves, and its area correct its evanescence; till a mere moment may become worth a millennium before; and the Transient may be to the large soul more than the Everlasting to the little: and then whether our Time be long or short by Sun and Moon we may well remain indifferent, since the life that is beyond time and nature is vivid within us.

When, therefore, in higher moments brought by the

sorrows of life, the tensions of duty, or the silence of thought, you catch some faint tones of a voice diviner than your own, know that you are not alone, and who it is that is with you. Stay not in the cold monologue of solitary meditation, but fling yourself into the communion of prayer. Fold not the personal shadows round you; lie open to the gleam that pierces them; confide in it as the brightest of realities, — a path of heavenly light streaking the troubled waters of your being, and leading your eye to the orb that sends it. —*James Martineau*.

The household to which the angel of death has come can never forget his coming. The shadow which his wings have cast over the soul must remain, however clearly the light from God's own love may shine.

Yes, when we are most perfectly resigned to his will, and most perfectly consoled under the loss by the dear promises of Christ, and most happy in the sweet hope of reunion with the dead, and most faithful in using the discipline which we know to be for our own good, the loss, in itself considered, may then seem, as it perhaps then becomes, greater than it ever was before. By the completeness of spiritual experience is the depth of our sorrow revealed. By the spiritual development of our affections the sacredness of earthly affection and of earthly relations is first discerned. A part of the blessing upon those who mourn comes by learning the greatness of their loss.

Hearts which rejoice cannot come so near to each other as hearts which grieve. Tears mingle more perfectly than smiles, and the chain of family love on earth becomes much stronger when some of its links are in heaven.

We need to learn that the purpose of the tree is to bear fruit, not flowers; and that the wisdom and goodness of God may abound only the more at the time when the blossoms fall. — *W. G. Eliot.*

And shall heaven have no children in it? Must none but gray hairs pass through its gates? Or shall not, rather, glad, gleesome children, with flowing hair and merry eyes, go with laughter through its doorways, to meet " their angels " who " do always behold the face of their Father in heaven "?

Let us not forget that there are two sides to dying, — this earth side and the heaven side. The stars that go out when morning comes do not stop shining; only some other eyes in some other land are made glad by them. — *M. J. Savage.*

> Yet Love will dream, and Faith will trust,
> (Since He who knows our need is just,)
> That somehow, somewhere, meet we must.
> Alas for him who never sees
> The stars shine through his cypress trees !
> Who, hopeless, lays his dead away,
> Nor looks to see the breaking day
> Across the mournful marbles play !
> Who hath not learned, in hours of faith,
>   The truth to flesh and sense unknown,
> That Life is ever Lord of Death,
>   And Love can never lose its own ! — *Whittier.*

If this life is all, there is no place for such a faculty as conscience with its lash of remorse in one hand, and its peace like a river, in the other. * * * * * The step from instinct to freedom and conscience, is a step from time to eternity. Conscience is not truly correlated to human life. The ethical implies the eternal.

If I were to construct one all-embracing argument for immortality, and were to put it into one word, it would be — *God.* * * * * * It was Christ's realization of the living God that rendered his own conviction of eternal life so absolute.

If the cup of life is full, there is little sense of past or future; the present is enough. * * * ⨍ When Christ speaks of eternal life, he does not mean future endless existence; this may be involved, but it is an inference or secondary thought; he means instead fullness or perfection of life. That it will go on forever, is a matter of course, but it is not the important feature of the truth. — *T. T. Munger.*

We talk of immortality; but there is a better phrase than that, — the word of Jesus, "eternal life." That implies not mere duration, but quality. It blends the present and the future in one. It sets before us a state into which we are called to enter now, and into which as we enter we find ourselves at home in our Father's house, beyond the power of doubt and fear.

Mere continuance of existence, — what is it? That bowlder yonder has existed for ages, a very eternity to the imagination; and it is only a bowlder after all. One hour of throbbing human life is worth more than its barren eternity. What is it to you or me whether we go on living, if life to us is made up of petty and ignoble thoughts and occupations? The real trouble with most of us is not the doubt whether we shall live hereafter, but the fact that as yet we have hardly begun to live at all.

Nothing is so completely beyond the power of death as a noble love. Parting can shatter only its outward shell. Under that strange touch, love in its inmost recesses kindles and glows with a divine fire. Whom of the living do we love as we love our dead? Whom else do we hold so sacredly and so surely? Not as a memory of a lost past, —nothing in our present is so real as they, and toward our unknown future we go with a great and solemn gladness, beckoned by their presence. — *Geo. S. Merriam.*

This is the change that comes. We are not afraid any more of our Father. We are not all happy. But if he says go, you will know that it is well, and you will not be afraid. You know it is the Father. Do not say God, that is far off — He is our Father.

And the little Pilgrim's voice echoed away through the great firmament to other worlds. And it breathed over the earth like some one saying Courage! to those whose hearts were failing; and it dropped down into the great confusion and traffic of the land of darkness, and startled many, like the voice of a child calling and calling, and never ceasing, Come! and come! and come! — *Mrs. Oliphant.*

> The leaves, though thick, are falling: one by one
> Decayed they drop from off their parent tree;
> Their work with Autumn's latest day is done, —
> Thou see'st them borne upon the breezes free.
> They lie strewn here and there, their many dyes
> That yesterday so caught thy passing eye;
> Soiled by the rain, each leaf neglected lies,
> Upon the path where now thou hurriest by.

Yet think thee not their beauteous tints less fair
  Than when they hung so gayly o'er thy head;
But rather find thee eyes, and look thee there
  Where now thy feet so heedless o'er them tread,
And thou shalt see, where wasting now they lie,
  The unseen hues of immortality. — *Jones Very*.

I do not say that death ends neither do I say that man is immortal. I say, I do not know. To know is one thing, to believe is another & to hope is still another. A hope for all good — for joy for all the children of men. I can say about immortality is there was a time when I was not that I was; now I am; and it may that it is no more wonderful that should continue forever now that have a start than it was that should begin. We love, & those we love die, & we cling to the hope, to the wish that we may meet them again. Love was the first to dream, and as long as we love we shall hope.

                    [Col. R. G. Ingersoll.]

Death,—in the death's eye is..
may we not discern him with-
ing? In that liveli
figured Sleep as in oration —..
over the beloved face which
knows thee no more, nor
canst for tears, the confluence
me with Eternity and come
in of the latter seeming love

OEMS.

DEATH.

Domini."

ngs,

wings,

's sun,
unfold,
eart of gold.
eet him,
:ord,—
th

Let us arise   et him;
Not in vain
Is the summons come for us to meet him;
He will stay,
And darken our sun;
He will stay
A desolate night, a weary day.
Since in that shadow our work is done,
And in that shadow our crowns are won,
Let us say still while his bitter chalice
Slowly into our hearts is poured,—
"Blessed is he that cometh
In the name of the Lord!"

Who is the Angel that cometh?
         Death!
But do not shudder and do not fear;
         Hold your breath,
For a kingly presence is drawing near,
         Cold and bright
         Is his flashing steel,
         Cold and bright
The smile that comes like a starry light
    To calm the terror and grief we feel;
    He comes to help and to save and to heal:
Then let us, baring our hearts and kneeling,
         Sing, while we wait this Angel's sword,—
         " Blessed is he that cometh
         In the name of the Lord!"

Adelaide Procter.

De Profundis.

The face which, duly as the sun,
Rose up for me with life begun,
To mark all bright hours of the day
With hourly love, is dimmed away, —
    And yet my days go on, go on.

The tongue which, like a stream, could run
Smooth music from the roughest stone,
And every morning with " Good day "
Make each day good, is hushed away, —
    And yet my days go on, go on.

The heart which, like a staff, was one
For mine to lean and rest upon;
The strongest on the longest day
With steadfast love, is caught away, —
    And yet my days go on, go on.

And cold before my summer's done,
And deaf in Nature's general tune,
And fallen too low for special fear,
And here, with hope no longer here, —
    While the tears drop, my days go on.

This Nature, though the snows be down,
Thinks kindly of the bird of June :
The little red hip on the tree
Is ripe for such.   What is for me,
  Whose days so winterly go on?

I ask less kindness to be done, —
Only to loose these pilgrim shoon,
(Too early worn and grimed) with sweet,
Cool, deathly touch to these tired feet,
  Till days go out which now go on.

A Voice reproves me thereupon,
More sweet than Nature's when the drone
Of bees is sweetest, and more deep
Than when the rivers overleap
  The shuddering pines, and thunder on.

God's Voice, not Nature's.   Night and noon
He sits upon the great white throne
And listens for the creature's praise.
What babble we of days and days?
  The Day-spring he, whose days go on.

He reigns above, he reigns alone ;
Systems burn out and leave his throne :
Fair mists of seraphs melt and fall
Around him, changeless amid all, —
  Ancient of days, whose days go on.

For us, — whatever's undergone,
Thou knowest, willest what is done.
Grief may be joy misunderstood ;
Only the Good discerns the good.
  I trust thee while my days go on.

Whatever's lost, it first was won :
We will not struggle nor impugn.
Perhaps the cup was broken here
That Heaven's new wine might show more clear.
  I praise thee while my days go on.

I praise thee while my days go on;
I love thee while my days go on;
Through dark and dearth, through fire and frost,
With emptied arms and treasure lost.
   I thank thee while my days go on.
                Elizabeth Barrett Browning.

Waiting by the Gate.

Beside a massive gateway built up in years gone by,
Upon whose top the clouds in eternal shadow lie,
While streams the evening sunshine on quiet wood and lea,
I stand and calmly wait till the hinges turn for me.

The tree-tops faintly rustle beneath the breeze's flight,
A soft and soothing sound, yet it whispers of the night;
I hear the wood-thrush piping one mellow descant more,
And scent the flowers that blow when the heat of day is o'er.

Behold, the portals open, and o'er the threshold, now,
There steps a weary one with a pale and furrowed brow;
His count of years is full, his allotted task is wrought;
He passes to his rest from a place that needs him not.

In sadness then I ponder how quickly fleets the hour
Of human strength and action, man's courage and his power.
I muse while still the wood-thrush sings down the golden day,
And as I look and listen the sadness wears away.

Again the hinges turn, and a youth, departing, throws
A look of longing backward, and sorrowfully goes;
A blooming maid, unbinding the roses from her hair,
Moves mournfully away from amid the young and fair.

O glory of our race that so suddenly decays!
O crimson flush of morning that darkens as we gaze!
O breath of summer blossoms that on the restless air
Scatters a moment's sweetness, and flies we know not where!

I grieve for life's bright promise, just shown and then withdrawn;
But still the sun shines round me : the evening bird sings on,
And I again am soothed, and, beside the ancient gate,
In the soft evening sunlight, I calmly stand and wait.

Once more the gates are opened; an infant group go out,
The sweet smile quenched forever, and stilled the sprightly shout.
O frail, frail tree of Life, that upon the greensward strows
Its fair young buds unopened, with every wind that blows !

So come from every region, so enter, side by side,
The strong and faint of spirit, the meek and men of pride.
Steps of earth's great and mighty, between those pillars gray,
And prints of little feet, mark the dust along the way.

And some approach the threshold whose looks are blank with fear,
And some whose temples brighten with joy in drawing near,
As if they saw dear faces, and caught the gracious eye
Of him, the Sinless Teacher, who came for us to die.

I mark the joy, the terror; yet these, within my heart,
Can neither wake the dread nor the longing to depart;
And, in the sunshine streaming on quiet wood and ,ea,
I calmly stand and wait till the hinges turn for me.

Bryant.

Suspiria.

Take them, O Death ! and bear away
   Whatever thou canst call thine own !
Thine image, stamped upon this clay,
   Doth give thee that, but that alone !

Take them, O Grave ! and let them lie
   Folded upon thy narrow shelves,
As garments by the soul laid by,
   And precious only to ourselves !

Take them, O great Eternity !
   Our little life is but a gust
That bends the branches of thy tree,
   And trails its blossoms in the dust !

Longfellow.

Dropping Down the River.

Dropping down the troubled river,
  To the tranquil, tranquil shore;
Dropping down the misty river,
Time's willow-shaded river,
  To the spring-embosomed shore;
Where the sweet light shineth ever,
  And the sun goes down no more;
  O wondrous, wondrous shore!

Dropping down the winding river,
  To the wide and welcome sea;
Dropping down the narrow river,
Man's weary, wayward river,
  To the blue and ample sea;
Where no tempest wrecketh ever,
  Where the sky is fair and free;
  O joyous, joyous sea!

Dropping down the noisy river,
  To our peaceful, peaceful home;
Dropping down the turbid river,
Earth's bustling, crowded river,
  To our gentle, gentle home:
Where the rough roar riseth never,
  And the vexings cannot come,
  O loved and longed-for home!

Dropping down the rapid river,
  To the dear and deathless land;
Dropping down the well-known river,
Life's swoln and rushing river
  To the resurrection-land;
Where the living live forever,
  And the dead have joined the band,
  In that fair and blessed land!

Horatius Bonar.

Here in an inn a stranger dwelt,
Here joy and grief by turns he felt;
Poor dwelling, now we close thy door,
  The talk is o'er,
The sojourner returns no more.

Now of a lasting home possessed,
He goes to seek a deeper rest.
Good-night! the day was sultry here,
  In toil and fear;
Good-night! the night is cool and clear.

Now open to us, gates of peace!
Here let the pilgrim's journey cease.
Ye quiet slumberers, make room
  In your still home,
For the new stranger who has come.

How many graves around us lie!
How many homes are in the sky!
Yes, for each saint doth Christ prepare
  A place with care;
Thy home is waiting, brother, there.

        F. Sachse.

Passing Away.

The fragrance of the rose,
Whose dewy leaves in morning's light unclose,
 Goes not more sweetly up
From its rich heart, as from an incense cup,
 Than thy freed spirit from its earthly shrine
 Passed with the still angel to the rest divine.

 Oh no! Thou didst not die!
Thou hast but lain the soul's frail vesture by,
 And soared to that pure height
Where day serene is followed by no night,
 And where the discipline of mortal woe
 No shadow over thee can ever throw.

Yet think thee not their beauteous tints less fair
  Than when they hung so gayly o'er thy head;
But rather find thee eyes, and look thee there
  Where now thy feet so heedless.o'er them tread,
And thou shalt see, where wasting now they lie,
  The unseen hues of immortality. — *Jones Very.*

I do not say that death ends all, neither do I say that man is immortal. I say I do not know. To know is one thing; to believe is another + to hope is still another. A hope for all good — for all joy for all the children of men. All I can say about immortality is this:— There was a time when I was not; after that I was; now I am; and it may be that it is no more wonderful that I should continue forever now that I have a start than it was that I should begin. We love, + those we love die, + we cling to the hope, to the wish that we may meet them again. Love was the first to dream, so long as we love we shall hope.

[Col. R. G. Ingersoll.]

Death,—in the Death of the Just,
may we not discern symbolic
ning? In that divinely
figured Sleep, as of Victory, rest-
over the beloved face which
knows thee no more, read (if
canst for tears) the confluence
me with Eternity, and some
ence of the latter peering thro'."

Pain !
Let us arise and go forth to greet him;
      Not in vain
Is the summons come for us to meet him;
      He will stay,
      And darken our sun ;
      He will stay
A desolate night, a weary day.
  Since in that shadow our work is done,
  And in that shadow our crowns are won,
Let us say still while his bitter chalice
    Slowly into our hearts is poured, —
     "Blessed is he that cometh
    In the name of the Lord !"

"Allah glorious!   Allah good!
Now thy world is understood;
Now the long, long wonder ends;
Yet ye weep, my erring friends,
While the man whom ye call dead,
In unspoken bliss, instead,
Lives and loves you, — lost, 'tis true,
By such light as shines for you;
But in the light ye cannot see
Of unfulfilled felicity, —
In a perfect paradise,
And a life that never dies.

"Farewell, friends!   Yet not farewell:
Where I am, ye, too, shall dwell.
I am gone before your face
A moment's time, a little space.
When ye come where I have stepped,
Ye will wonder why ye wept;
Ye will know, by wise love taught,
That here is all, and there is naught.
Weep awhile, if ye are fain:
Sunshine still must follow rain;
Only not at death, — for death,
Now I know, is that first breath
Which our souls draw when we enter
Life, which is of all life centre.

"Be ye certain all seems love,
Viewed from Allah's throne above;
Be ye stout of heart, and come
Bravely onward to your home!
La Allah illa Allah! yea!
Thou Love divine!   Thou Love alway!"

He that died at Azan gave
This to those who made his grave.

                                        Edwin Arnold.

Here and There.

A little fold of hands,
A little drop of sands,
And the freed spirit stands
  Beyond the veil victorious;
Where the sands of life ne'er run,
And the day is never done,
Eternity is won,
  Eternity all glorious.

Ye, who within life's slow
And long procession go,
Who 'mid the sullen flow
  Of storms and tempests wander, --
Ye name me Death!   Ye call
Me cursed for the pall
That once must fold o'er all —
  Birth, they have named me yonder!

Joshua Swan.

Invocation.

Answer me, burning stars of night!
  Where is the spirit gone,
That past the reach of human sight
  As a swift breeze hath flown?
And the stars answered me: " We roll
  In light and power on high;
But, of the never-dying soul,
  Ask that which cannot die."

O many-toned and changeless wind!
  Thou art a wanderer free;
Tell me, if thou its place canst find,
  Far over mount and sea?
And the wind murmured in reply:
  " The blue deep I have crossed,
And met its barks and billows high,
  But not what thou hast lost."

Ye clouds that gorgeously repose
  Around the setting sun,
Answer! have ye a home for those
  Whose earthly race is run?
The bright clouds answered: " We depart,
  We vanish from the sky;
Ask what is deathless in thy heart
  For that which cannot die."

Speak then, thou voice of God within,
  Thou of the deep, low tone!
Answer me, through life's restless din —
  Where is the spirit flown?
And the voice answered: " Be thou still!
  Enough to know is given:
Clouds, winds, and stars their part fulfil —
  Thine is to trust in Heaven."

                                    Mrs. Hemans.

Absence.

What shall I do with all the days and hours
  That must be counted ere I see thy face?
How shall I charm the interval that lowers
  Between this time and that sweet time of grace?

I'll tell thee : for thy sake, I will lay hold
  Of all good aims, and consecrate to thee,
In worthy deeds, each moment that is told
  While thou, beloved one, art far from me.

For thee, I will arouse my thoughts to try
  All heavenward flights, all high and holy strains;
For thy dear sake, I will walk patiently
  Through these long hours, nor call their minutes pains.

I will this weary blank of absence make
  A noble task-time, and will therein strive
To follow excellence, and to o'ertake
  More good than I have won since yet I live.

Into the Silent Land!
To you, ye boundless regions
Of all perfection!   Tender morning visions
Of beauteous souls!   The Future's pledge and band!
Who in life's battle firm doth stand,
Shall bear Hope's tender blossoms
Into the Silent Land!

O Land!   O Land!
For all the broken-hearted
The mildest herald by our fate allotted,
Beckons, and with inverted torch doth stand
To lead us with a gentle hand
To the land of the great Departed,
Into the Silent Land!

From the German of Salis.

Longfellow.

The Future.

What may we take into the vast Forever?
That marble door
Admits no fruit of all our long endeavor,
No fame-wreathed crown we wore,
No garnered lore.

What can we bear beyond the unknown portal?
No gold, no gains
Of all our toiling : in the life immortal
No hoarded wealth remains,
Nor gilds, nor stains.

Naked from out that far abyss behind us
We entered here :
No word came with our coming, to remind us
What wondrous world was near,
No hope, no fear.

Into the silent, starless night before us,
Naked we glide :
No hand has mapped the constellations o'er us,
No comrade at our side,
No chart, no guide.

Yet fearless toward the midnight black and hollow,
    Our footsteps fare:
The beckoning of a Father's hand we follow —
    His love alone is there,
    No curse, no care.

                E. R. Sill.

From the German of Leopold Schefer

All that God wounds he constantly is healing,
Quietly, gently, softly, but most surely;
He helps the lowliest herb, with wounded stalk,
To rise again.
Deep in the treasure-house of wealthy Nature,
A ready instinct works and moves
To clothe the naked sparrow in the nest,
Or trim the plumage of an aged raven;
Yes, in the slow decaying of a rose,
God works as well as in the unfolding bud;
He works with gentleness unspeakable
In Death itself; a thousand times more careful
Than even the mother by her sick child watching.

The Choir Invisible.

Oh may I join the choir invisible
Of those immortal dead who live again
In minds made better by their presence; live
In pulses stirred to generosity,
In deeds of daring rectitude, in scorn
Of miserable aims that end in self,
In thoughts sublime that pierce the night like stars,
And with their mild persistence urge men's minds
To vaster issues.
          So to live is heaven:
To make undying music in the world,
Breathing as beauteous order, that controls
With growing sway the growing life of man.

This is life to come,
Which martyred men have made more glorious
For us who strive to follow.   May I reach
That purest heaven ; be to other souls
The cup of strength in some great agony ;
Enkindle generous ardor ; feed pure love ;
Beget the smiles that have no cruelty ;
Be the sweet presence of a good diffused,
And in diffusion ever more intense.
So shall I join the choir invisible,
Whose music is the gladness of the world.

George Eliot.

Life.

Life ! I know not what thou art,
But know that thou and I must part ;
And when, or how, or where we met,
I own to me 's a secret yet.

Life ! we've been long together,
Through pleasant and through cloudy weather ;
'Tis hard to part when friends are dear,—
Perhaps 't will cost a sigh, a tear ;
Then steal away, give little warning,
        Choose thine own time ;
Say not Good Night, — but in some brighter clime
        Bid me Good Morning.

Anna L. Barbauld.

In Memoriam.

Farewell ! since nevermore for thee
    The sun comes up our eastern skies,
Less bright henceforth shall sunshine be
    To some fond hearts and saddened eye

There are, who for thy last, long sleep,
    Shall sleep as sweetly nevermore ;
Shall weep because thou canst not weep,
    And grieve that all thy griefs are o'er.

R. J.

Prospice.

Fear death ? — to feel the fog in my throat,
    The mist in my face,
When the snows begin, and the blasts denote
    I am nearing the place,
The power of the night, the press of the storm,
    The post of the foe ;
Where he stands, the Arch Fear, in a visible form,
    Yet the strong man must go :
For the journey is done, and the summit attained,
    And the barriers fall,
Though a battle 's to fight ere the guerdon be gained,
    The reward of it all.

    .   .   .   .

For sudden the worst turns the best to the brave,
    The black minute 's at end,
And the element's rage, the fiend-voices that rave,
    Shall dwindle, shall blend,
Shall change, shall become first a peace out of pain,
    Then a light, then thy breast, —
O thou soul of my soul ! I shall clasp thee again,
    And with God be the rest !

                          Robert Browning.

From the "Threnody."

Wilt thou not ope thy heart to know
What rainbows teach, and sunsets show ?
Verdict which accumulates
From lengthening scroll of human fates,
Voice of earth to earth returned,
Prayers of saints that inly burned, —
Saying, *What is excellent,*
As God lives, is permanent ;
Hearts are dust, hearts' loves remain ;
Hearts' love will meet thee again.
Revere the Maker ; fetch thine eye
Up to his style, and manners of the sky.

PART II.

RESIGNATION—TRUST.

Ministering Angels.

Brother, the angels say,
  Peace to thy heart!
We, too, O brother, have
  Been as thou art,—
Hope-lifted, doubt-depressed,
  Seeing in part;
Tried, troubled, tempted,
  Sustained, as thou art.

Brother, they softly say,
  Be our thoughts one;
Bend thou with us and pray,
  "Thy will be done!"
Our God is thy God;
  He willeth the best;
Trust him as we trusted;
  Rest as we rest!

Ye, too, they gently say,
  Shall angels be;
Ye, too, O brothers,
  From earth shall be free:
Yet in earth's loved ones
  Ye still shall have part,
Bearing God's strength and love
  To the torn heart.

Thus when the spirit, tried,
  Tempted, and worn,
Finding no earthly aid,
  Heavenward doth turn,
Come these sweet angel-tones,
  Falling like balm,
And on the troubled heart
  Steals a deep calm.

Hymns of the Spirit.

"Not as I will."

Blindfolded and alone I stand
With unknown thresholds on each hand;
The darkness deepens as I grope,
Afraid to fear, afraid to hope;
Yet this one thing I learn to know
Each day more surely as I go,
That doors are opened, ways are made,
Burdens are lifted, or are laid,
By some great law, unseen and still,
Unfathomed purpose to fulfil,
    "Not as I will."

Blindfolded and alone I wait,
Loss seems too bitter, gain too late;
Too heavy burdens in the load,
And too few helpers on the road;
And joy is weak and grief is strong,
And years and days so long, so long:
Yet this one thing I learn to know
Each day more surely as I go,
That I am glad the good and ill
By changeless law is ordered still,
    "Not as I will."

"Not as I will:" the sound grows sweet
Each time my lips the words repeat;
"Not as I will:" the darkness feels
More safe than light, when this thought steals

Wherefore, O heart, no longer say
Dust unto dust our own we lay,
Ashes to ashes leave to-day,

But with a faith set heavenward
Say, Life to life we have restored,
Spirit to spirit, God to God.

John Tunis.

Sometime.

Sometime, when all life's lessons have been learned,
   And sun and stars for evermore have set,
The things which our weak judgment here have spurned,
   The things o'er which we grieved with lashes wet,
Will flash before us, out of life's dark night,
   As stars shine most in deeper tints of blue;
And we shall see how all God's plans were right,
   And how what seemed reproof was love most true.

And we shall see how, while we frown and sigh,
   God's plans go on as best for you and me;
How, when we called, he heeded not our cry,
   Because his wisdom to the end could see.
And e'en as prudent parents disallow
   Too much of sweet to craving babyhood,
So God, perhaps, is keeping from us now
   Life's sweetest things, because it seemeth good.

And if, sometimes, commingled with life's wine,
   We find the wormwood, and rebel and shrink,
Be sure a wiser hand than yours or mine
   Pours out this potion for our lips to drink.
And if some friend we love is lying low,
   Where human kisses cannot reach his face,
Oh, do not blame the loving Father so,
   But wear your sorrow with obedient grace!

And you will shortly know that lengthened breath
  Is not the sweetest gift God sends his friends,
And that, sometimes, the sable pall of death
  Conceals the fairest boon his love can send.
If we could push ajar the gates of life,
  And stand within, and all God's workings see,
We could interpret all this doubt and strife,
  And for each mystery could find a key!

But not to-day. Then be content, poor heart!
  God's plans, like lilies, pure and white unfold;
We must not tear the close-shut leaves apart,
  Time will reveal the chalices of gold.

while

And, through patient toil, we reach the land
  Where tired feet, with sandals loosed, may rest,
When we shall clearly know and understand,
  I think that we will say, "God knew the best!"

                                    May Riley Smith.

Yet a Little While.

Oh! for the peace which floweth as a river,
  Making life's desert places bloom and smile.
Oh! for a faith to grasp heaven's bright forever
  Amid the shadows of earth's "little while."

A little while for patient vigil-keeping,
  To face the storm, to wrestle with the strong;
A little while to sow the seed with weeping,
  Then bind the sheaves, and sing the harvest-song.

A little while midst shadow and illusion,
  To strive, by faith, love's mysteries to spell;
Then read each dark enigma's bright solution,
  Then hail sight's verdict, "He doth all things well!"

And he who is himself the Gift and Giver,
  The future glory and the present smile,
With the bright promise of the glad "forever"
  Will light the shadows of the "little while."

                                    Jane Crewdson.

Out of the Depths.

Thou that art strong to comfort, look on me!
  I sit in darkness, and behold no light!
Over my heart the waves of agony
  Have gone and left me faint!   Forbear to smite
A bruised and broken reed!   Sustain, sustain,
  Divinest Comforter, to thee I fly;
Let me not fly in vain!
  Support me with thy love, or else I die!
Whate'er I had was thine!
  A God of mercy thou hast ever been;
Assist me to resign,
  And if I murmur, count it not for sin!
How rich I was, I dare not — dare not think;
How poor I am, thou knowest, who can see
Into my soul's unfathomed misery;
  Forgive me if I shrink!
Forgive me if I shed these human tears,
That it so hard appears
To yield my will to thine, forgive, forgive!
  Father, it is a bitter cup to drink!

My soul is strengthened! it shall bear
  My lot, whatever it may be;
And from the depths of my despair
  I will look up and trust in thee!

                              Mary Howitt.

Resting in God.

  Since thy Father's arm sustains thee,
          Peaceful be;
  When a chastening hand restrains thee,
          It is he.
  Know his love in full completeness
  Fills the measure of thy weakness;
  If he wound thy spirit sore,
          Trust him more.

Without murmur, uncomplaining,
    In his hand
Leave whatever things thou canst not
    Understand.
Though the world thy folly spurneth,
From thy faith in pity turneth,
Peace thy inmost soul shall fill,
    Lying still.

Fearest sometimes that thy Father
    Hath forgot ?
When the clouds around thee gather
    Doubt him not.
Always hath the daylight broken, —
Always hath he comfort spoken, —
Better hath he been for years
    Than thy fears.

Therefore, whatsoe'er betideth,
    Night or day, —
Know his love for thee provideth
    Good alway.
Crown of sorrow gladly take,
Grateful wear it for his sake ;
Sweetly bending to his will,
    Lying still.

To his own thy Father giveth
    Daily strength ;
To each troubled soul that liveth,
    Peace at length.
Weakest lambs have largest share
Of this tender Shepherd's care ;
Ask him not, then, " when ? " or " how ? "
    Only bow.

Charles R. Hagenbach.

Sits upon the grave and sings it,
  Sings it when the heart would groan,
Sings it when the shadows darken,
  "It is better farther on."

Farther on ? Oh! how much farther ?
  Count the mile-stones one by one.
No! no counting — only trusting
  "It is better farther on!"

Anonymous.

Prayer for Strength.

Father, before thy footstool kneeling,
  Once more my heart goes up to thee,
For aid, for strength to thee appealing,
  Thou who alone canst succor me.

Hear me ! for heart and flesh are failing,
  My spirit yielding in the strife;
And anguish, wild as unavailing,
  Sweeps in a flood across my life.

Help me to stem the tide of sorrow;
  Help me to bear thy chastening rod;
Give me endurance; let me borrow
  Strength from thy promise, O my God!

Not mine the grief which words may lighten;
  Not mine the tears of common woe:
The pang with which my heart-strings tighten,
  Only the All-seeing One may know.

And oh! in my exceeding weakness,
  Make thy strength perfect; thou art strong:
Aid me to do thy will with meekness, —
  Thou, to whom all my powers belong.

Oh! let me feel that thou art near me;
  Close to thy side, I shall not fear:
Hear me, O Strength of Israel, hear me !
  Sustain and aid! in mercy hear!

Anonymous.

No More Sea.

Life of our life, and Light of all our seeing,
  How shall we rest on any hope but thee?
What time our souls, to thee for refuge fleeing,
  Long for the home where there is no more sea?

For still this sea of life, with endless wailing,
  Dashes above our heads its blinding spray,
And vanquished hearts, sick with remorse and failing,
  Moan like the waves at set of autumn day.

And ever round us swells the insatiate ocean
  Of sin and doubt that lures us to our grave;
When its wild billows, with their mad commotion,
  Would sweep us down — then only thou canst save.

And deep and dark the fearful gloom unlighted
  Of that untried and all-surrounding sea,
On whose bleak shore arriving — lone — benighted,
  We fall and lose ourselves at last — in thee.

Yea! in thy life our little lives are ended,
  Into thy depths our trembling spirits fall;
In thee enfolded, gathered, comprehended,
  As holds the sea her waves — thou hold'st us all!
                                    Eliza Scudder.

The Eternal Goodness.

Within the maddening maze of things,
  And tossed by storm and flood,
To one fixed stake my spirit clings:
  I know that God is good.

I long for household voices gone,
  For vanished smiles I long;
But God hath led my dear ones on,
  And he can do no wrong.

Enough that blessings undeserved
   Have marked my erring track ; —
That wheresoe'er my feet have swerved,
   His chastening turned me back ; —

That more and more a Providence
   Of love is understood,
Making the springs of time and sense
   Sweet with eternal good ; —

That death seems but a covered way
   Which opens into light,
Wherein no blinded child can stray
   Beyond the Father's sight ; —

That care and trial seem at last,
   Through Memory's sunset air,
Like mountain ranges overpast,
   In purple distance fair ; —

That all the jarring notes of life
   Seem blending in a psalm,
And all the angles of its strife
   Slow rounding into calm.

And so the shadows fall apart,
   And so the west winds play ;
And all the windows of my heart
   I open to the day.
                      J. G. Whittier.

Death of a Sister.

I will not mock thee with the poor world's common
   And heartless phrase,
Nor wrong the memory of a sainted woman
   With idle praise.

With silence only as their benediction,
   God's angels come
Where, in the shadow of a great affliction,
   The soul sits dumb !

Yet would I say what thy own heart approveth;
    Our Father's will,
Calling to him the dear one whom he loveth,
    Is mercy still.

God calls our loved ones, but we lose not wholly
    What he hath given;
They live on earth, in thought and deed, as truly
    As in his heaven.

Up, then, my brother! Lo, the fields of harvest
    Lie white in view!
She lives and loves thee, and the God thou servest
    To both is true.
                       J. G. Whittier.

PART III.

A GOOD LIFE.

From the "Elegy on the Death of Dr. Channing."

I do not come to weep above thy pall,
  And mourn the dying out of noble powers;
The poet's clearer eye should see, in all
  Earth's seeming woe, the seed of Heaven's flowers.

Truth needs no champions : in the infinite deep
  Of everlasting Soul her strength abides;
From Nature's heart her mighty pulses leap,
  Through Nature's veins her strength, undying, tides.

Peace is more strong than war, and gentleness,
  Where force were vain, makes conquest o'er the wave;
And love lives on and hath a power to bless,
  When they who loved are hidden in the grave.

No power can die that ever wrought for Truth;
  Thereby a law of Nature it became,
And lives unwithered in its sinewy youth,
  When he who called it forth is but a name.

Therefore I cannot think thee wholly gone;
  The better part of thee is with us still;
The soul its hampering clay aside hath thrown,
  And only freer wrestles with the Ill.

Thou livest in the life of all good things;
  What words thou spak'st for Freedom shall not die;
Thou sleepest not, for now thy Love hath wings
  To soar where hence thy Hope could hardly fly.

(157)

And often, from that other world, on this
   Some gleams from great souls gone before may shine,
To shed on struggling hearts a clearer bliss,
   And clothe the Right with lustre more divine.

Thou art not idle : in thy higher sphere
   Thy spirit bends itself to loving tasks,
And strength to perfect what it dreamed of here
   Is all the crown and glory that it asks.

For sure, in Heaven's wide chambers, there is room
   For love and pity, and for helpful deeds ;
Else were our summons thither but a doom
   To life more vain than this in clayey weeds.

Farewell ! good man, good angel now ! this hand
   Soon, like thine own, shall lose its cunning too ;
Soon shall this soul, like thine, bewildered stand,
   Then leap to thread the free, unfathomed blue.

This laurel-leaf I cast upon thy bier ;
   Let worthier hands than these thy wreath entwine ;
Upon thy hearse I shed no useless tear, —
   For us weep rather thou in calm divine !
                         J. R. Lowell.

Well Done.

Servant of God, well done !   They serve God well,
Who serve his creatures ; when the funeral bell
Tolls for the dead, there 's nothing left of all
That decks the scutcheon and the velvet pall
Save this.   The coronet is empty show :
The strength and loveliness are hid below :
The shifting wealth to others hath accrued :
And learning cheers not the grave's solitude :
What's done, is what remains !   Ah, blessed they
Who leave completed tasks of love to stay
And answer mutely for them, being dead :
Life was not purposeless, though Life be fled.
                    Caroline Norton.
                    The Lady of La Garaye.

To J. S.

God gives us love.   Something to love
  He lends us ; but, when love is grown
To ripeness, that on which it throve
  Falls off, and love is left alone.

And though mine own eyes fill with dew,
  Drawn from the spirit through the brain,
I will not even preach to you,
  " Weep, weeping dulls the inward pain."

I will not say " God's ordinance
  Of death is blown in every wind ; "
For that is not a common chance
  That takes away a noble mind.

Sleep sweetly, tender heart, in peace ;
  Sleep, holy spirit, blessed soul,
While the stars burn, the moons increase,
  And the great ages onward roll.

Sleep till the end, true soul and sweet,
  Nothing comes to thee new or strange ;
Sleep full of rest from head to feet ;
  Lie still, dry dust, secure of change.

                  Alfred Tennyson.

G. L. S.

He has done the work of a true man, —
  Crown him, honor him, love him.
Weep over him, tears of woman,
  Stoop, manliest brows, above him !

For the warmest of hearts is frozen,
  The freest of hands is still ;
And the gap in our picked and chosen
  The long years may not fill.

No duty could overtask him,
  No need his will outrun;
Or ever our lips could ask him,
  His hands the work had done.

He forgot his own soul for others,
  Himself to his neighbor lending;
He found the Lord in his suffering brothers,
  And not in the clouds descending.

Ah, well! — The world is discreet;
  There are plenty to pause and wait;
But here was a man who set his feet
  Sometimes in advance of fate

Never rode to the wrong's redressing
  A worthier paladin;
Shall he not hear the blessing,
  " Good and faithful, enter in!"

J. G. Whittier.

A Memorial.

Oh, thicker, deeper, darker growing,
  The solemn vista to the tomb
Must know henceforth another shadow,
  And give another cypress room.

To homely joys and loves and friendships
  Thy genial nature fondly clung;
And so the shadow on the dial
  Ran back and left thee always young.

And who could blame the generous weakness,
  Which, only to thyself unjust,
So overprized the worth of others,
  And dwarfed thy own with self-distrust?

All hearts grew warmer in the presence
  Of one who, seeking not his own,
Gave freely for the love of giving,
  Nor reaped for self the harvest sown.

Thy greeting smile was pledge and prelude
　Of generous deeds and kindly words;
In thy large heart were fair guest-chambers,
　Open to sunrise and the birds!

The task was thine to mould and fashion
　Life's plastic newness into grace;
To make the boyish heart heroic,
　And light with thought the maiden's face.

O'er all the land in town and prairie,
　With bended heads of mourning, stand
The living forms that owe their beauty
　And fitness to thy shaping hand.

O friend! if thought and sense avail not
　To know thee henceforth as thou art,
That all is well with thee forever
　I trust the instincts of my heart.

Thine be the quiet habitations,
　Thine the green pastures, blossom-sown,
And smiles of saintly recognition
　As sweet and tender as thy own.

Thou com'st not from the hush and shadow
　To meet us, but to thee we come;
With thee we never can be strangers,
　And where thou art must still be home.

J. G. Whittier.

E. S. G.

"At eve there shall be light," the promise runs
　In the dear volume that he loved so well;
Ay, and for him the promise was fulfilled,
　When rang for him the solemn vesper-bell.

His was no day of sweet, unsullied blue,
　And bright, warm sunshine on the grass and flowers;
But many a cloud of loss and grief and pain
　Dropped its deep shadow on the fleeting hours.

For still, though hours were his, serene and still,
  And radiant hours of steady glowing noon,
That cloud of pain was ever near to touch
  With quivering sadness every brightest boon.

And, as his afternoon drew on to eve
  And still he lingered in the whitened field,
The reapers were so few, till night should fall
  Fain would his hand the heavy sickle wield, —

Darker it grew and darker o'er the land,
  And he was forced to lay the sickle by;
But did it brighten, then his hand was quick
  To seize once more its opportunity.

So the day faded, and the evening came;
  Then from the sky the clouds were furled away,
And a great peace and beauty welcómed in
  The evening star with her benignant ray.

And all the air was hushed and whispering,
  And all the sky was purely, softly bright;
And so the blessed promise was fulfilled;
  " At eve," it said, — " at eve there shall be light."

But that fair evening did not end in night,
  With shadows deep, and darkness all forlorn,
Just at its brightest he was snatched away
  Into the golden palaces of morn.

And surely since the Master went that way,
  To welcome there earth's holiest and best,
He has not welcomed one who loved him more
  Than he who leaned that evening on his breast.

                             J. W. Chadwick.

In Memory of the Lady Augusta Stanley.

O blessed life of service and of love!
  Heart wide as life, deep as life's deepest woe;
God's servants serve him day and night above,
  Thou servedst day and night, we thought, below.

Hands full of blessings, lavished far and wide,
  Hands tender to bind up hearts wounded sore;
Stooping quite down earth's lowest needs beside, —
  Master, like thee ! we thought, and said no more.

We o'er all sorrow would have raised thee up,
  Crowned with life's choicest blossoms night and morn;
God made thee drink of his beloved's cup,
  And crowned thee with the Master's crown of thorn.

Looking from thee to him, once wounded sore,
  We learned a little more his face to see;
Then looking from the cross for us he bore,
  To thine, we almost understood for thee !

Till now, again ! we gaze on thee above,
  Strong and unwearied, serving day and night;
O blessed life of service and of love !
  Master, like thee, and with thee in thy light !
                                    Elizabeth Charles.

Charles Lowe.

"If ye love me," Jesus said,
Just before his spirit sped,
"Ye would all rejoice, for know
To my Father I shall go."

As we loved our brother here,
We will check the starting tear,
And rejoice that soul new-born
To his Father now has gone.

Thanks to God for life so pure,
Strong to do, to bear, endure;
Thanks for faith that feared no cross,
Thanks for hope that knew no loss.

Thanks for love so deep and strong,
Love of right and hate of wrong;
Love, unwelcome truth could tell
Just because it loved so well.

Love embracing in its span
Truth and right, and God and man;
Love so loyal and so sweet
It could every duty meet.

Love that cast out every fear,
As the parting hour drew near;
Love that clasped the Father's hand,
Leading to the brighter land.

Risen brother! from above
Let us all still feel thy love;
Earth was fairer for thy stay,
Heaven is nearer us to-day.

W. P. Tilden.

From " Rugby Chapel."

O strong soul, by what shore
Tarriest thou now? For that force,
Surely, has not been left vain!
Somewhere, surely, afar,
In the sounding labor-house vast
Of being is practised that strength,
Zealous, beneficent, firm!

Yes, in some far-shining sphere,
Conscious or not of the past,
Still thou performest the word
Of the Spirit in whom thou dost live —
Prompt, unwearied, as here!
Still thou upraisest with zeal
The humble good from the ground,
Sternly repressest the bad!
Still, like a trumpet, dost rouse
Those who with half-open eyes
Tread the border-land dim
'Twixt vice and virtue; reviv'st,
Succourest! — this was thy work,
This was thy life upon earth.

Servants of God ! — or sons
Shall I not call you ? because
Not as servants ye knew
Your Father's innermost mind,
His, who unwillingly sees
One of his little ones lost —
Yours is the praise, if mankind
Hath not as yet in its march
Fainted, and fallen, and died !

See ! In the rocks of the world
Marches the host of mankind,
A feeble, wavering line.
Where are they tending ? — A God
Marshalled them, gave them their goal. —
Ah, but the way is so long !
Then, in such hour of need
Of your fainting, dispirited race,
Ye, like angels appear,
Radiant with ardor divine.
Beacons of hope, ye appear !
Languor is not in your heart,
Weakness is not in your word,
Weariness not on your brow.
Ye alight in our van ! at your voice,
Panic, despair, flee away.
Ye move through the ranks, recall
The stragglers, refresh the outworn,
Praise, re-inspire the brave.
Order, courage, return ;
Eyes rekindling, and prayers,
Follow your steps as ye go.
Ye fill up the gaps in our files,
Strengthen the wavering line,
Stablish, continue our march,
On, to the bound of the waste,
On, to the City of God.

Matthew Arnold.

PART IV.

SUFFERING AND REST.

The Sleep.

" He giveth His beloved sleep." *Ps. cxxvii : 2.*

Of all the thoughts of God that are
Borne inward unto souls afar,
Along the Psalmist's music deep,
  Now tell me if that any is,
  For gift or grace, surpassing this —
" He giveth his beloved, sleep " ?

What would we give to our beloved ?
The hero's heart to be unmoved,
The poet's star-tuned harp to sweep,
  The patriot's voice to teach and rouse,
  The monarch's crown to light the brows ?
" He giveth his beloved, sleep."

What do we give to our beloved ?
A little faith all undisproved,
A little dust to overweep,
  And bitter memories to make
  The whole earth blasted for our sake.
" He giveth his beloved, sleep."

" Sleep soft, beloved ! " we sometimes say,
But have no tune to charm away
Sad dreams that through the eyelids creep ;
  But never doleful dream again
  Shall break the happy slumber, when
  " He giveth his beloved, sleep."

Sleep, lovely one, sleep!
Earth's beauty is a summer sunset's glow,
Fading to darkness as the night shades grow;
Thy beauty was of climes we do not know.
Sleep, lovely one, sleep!

Sleep, loving one, sleep!
Warm hearts and tender cluster, true and kind;
Thy sorrowing ones they shall not fail to find;
Love well shall guard the love thou leav'st behind.
Sleep, loving one, sleep!

Sleep, beloved one, sleep!
That only asks to rest,
Unquestioning, upon
A loving breast.

My good right hand forgets
Its cunning now;
To march the weary march
I know not how.

He sees when their footsteps falter, when their hearts grow weak and
faint;
He marks when their strength is failing, and listens to each com-
plaint;
He bids them rest for a season, for the path-way has grown too steep;
And folded in fair green pastures, he giveth his loved ones sleep.

Like weary and worn-out children, that sigh for the daylight's close,
He knows that they oft are longing for home and its sweet repose;
So he calls them in from their labors ere the shadows around them
creep,
And silently watching o'er them, he giveth his loved ones sleep.

PART IV.

SUFFERING AND REST.

The Sleep.

" He giveth His beloved sleep." Ps. cxxvii : 2.

Of all the thoughts of God that are
Borne inward unto souls afar,
Along the Psalmist's music deep,
　Now tell me if that any is,
　For gift or grace, surpassing this —
" He giveth his beloved, sleep " ?

What would we give to our beloved ?
The hero's heart to be unmoved,
The poet's star-tuned harp to sweep,
　The patriot's voice to teach and rouse,
　The monarch's crown to light the brows ?
" He giveth his beloved, sleep."

What do we give to our beloved ?
A little faith all undisproved,
A little dust to overweep,
　And bitter memories to make
　The whole earth blasted for our sake.
" He giveth his beloved, sleep."

" Sleep soft, beloved ! " we sometimes say,
But have no tune to charm away
Sad dreams that through the eyelids creep ;
　But never doleful dream again
　Shall break the happy slumber, when
" He giveth his beloved, sleep."

Sleep, lovely one, sleep!
Earth's beauty is a summer sunset's glow,
Fading to darkness as the night shades grow;
Thy beauty was of climes we do not know.
Sleep, lovely one, sleep!

Sleep, loving one, sleep!
Warm hearts and tender cluster, true and kind;
Thy sorrowing ones they shall not fail to find;
Love well shall guard the love thou leav'st behind.
Sleep, loving one, sleep!

Sleep, beloved one, sleep!
. . . memory in our hearts abides;
That only asks to rest, swiftly glides,
Unquestioning, upon
A loving breast.

My good right hand forgets
Its cunning now;
To march the weary march
I know not how.

Potter.)

He sees when their footsteps . . . ow weak and
faint;
He marks when their strength is failing, and listens to each com-
plaint;
He bids them rest for a season, for the path-way has grown too steep;
And folded in fair green pastures, he giveth his loved ones sleep.

Like weary and worn-out children, that sigh for the daylight's close,
He knows that they oft are longing for home and its sweet repose;
So he calls them in from their labors ere the shadows around them
creep,
And silently watching o'er them, he giveth his loved ones sleep.

He giveth it, oh! so gently, as a mother will hush to rest
The babe that she softly pillows so tenderly on her breast;
Forgotten are now the trials and sorrows that made them weep,
For with many a soothing promise, he giveth his loved ones sleep.

He giveth it!   Friends the dearest can never this boon bestow;
But he touches the drooping eyelids, and placid the features grow;
Their foes may gather about them, and storms may round them sweep,
But, guarding them safe from danger, he giveth his loved ones sleep.

All dread of the distant future, all fears that oppressed to-day,
Like mists that clear in the sunlight, have noiselessly passed away;
Nor call, nor clamor can rouse them from slumbers so pure and deep,
For only his voice can reach them, who giveth his loved ones sleep.

Weep not that their toils are over, weep not that their race is run;
God grant we may rest as calmly when our work, like theirs, is done!
Till then we would yield with gladness our treasures to him to keep,
And rejoice in the sweet assurance, he giveth his loved ones sleep.

Anonymous.

Our Home Maker.

Where the mountains slope to the westward,
    And their purple chalices hold
The new made wine of the sunset —
    Crimson and amber and gold —

In this old, wide-opened doorway,
    With the elm-boughs over head—
The house all garnished behind her,
    And the plentiful table spread.—

She has stood to welcome our coming,
    Watching our upward climb,
In the sweet June weather that brought us,
    Oh, many and many a time!

To-day, in the gentle splendor
    Of the early summer noon —
Perfect in sunshine and fragrance
    Although it is hardly June —,

SUFFERING AND REST. 181

And we, because we shared his love,
  May cherish the uplifting hope
. That life to us is more, by just
His altitude above our dust.
More by the power he has attained
  To minister as angels may;
More by the knowledge he has gained
  Of love's supremest, patient way;
Of blessing through the cloud or sun,
So one all-perfect Will be done.

And he (the thought is radiant) he
  This very moment may be near,
With solace meted soothingly
  To feed a hope or hush a fear:
So true it is, divinest things
Come borne to us on hidden wings.

So well we knew our Father's care
  Hovers about us, night and day,
So sweet it is to think the air
  Is moved in a mysterious way
By breath of one beloved on earth
Grown lovelier by celestial birth.

Then say not he is of the dead,
  'Tis only we in cerements dim,
Who fail of life around, o'erhead;
  But say it nevermore of him
Whom death to livelier joys has called,
Who lives among us disenthralled.

                    Mary B. Dodge.

The Conqueror's Grave.

Within this lowly grave a conqueror lies,

Tired Out.

He does well who does his best;
Is he weary? let him rest.
Brothers! I have done my best,
I am weary — let me rest.

He giveth it, oh! so gently, as a mother will hush to rest
The babe that she softly pillows so tenderly on her breast;
Forgotten are now the trials and sorrows that made them weep,
For with many a soothing promise, he giveth his loved ones sleep.

He giveth it! Friends the dearest can never this boon bestow;
But he touches the drooping eyelids, and placid the features grow;
Their foes may gather about them, and storms may round them sweep,
But, guarding them safe from danger, he giveth his loved ones sleep.

All dread of the distant future, all fears that oppressed to-day,
Like mists that clear in the sunlight, have noiselessly passed away;
Nor call, nor clamor can rouse them from slumbers so pure and deep,
For only his voice can reach them, who giveth his loved ones sleep.

Weep not that their toils are over, weep not that their race is run;
God grant we may rest as calmly when our work, like theirs, is done!
Till then we would yield with gladness our treasures to him to keep,
And rejoice in the sweet assurance, he giveth his loved ones sleep.

Anonymous.

Our Home Maker.

Where the mountains slope to the westward,
  And their purple chalices hold
The new made wine of the sunset —
  Crimson and amber and gold —

In this old, wide-opened doorway,
  With the elm-boughs over head —
The house all garnished behind her,
  And the plentiful table spread —

She has stood to welcome our coming,
  Watching our upward climb,

Made in the image of the Lord,
  An effluence from the central light,
An inbreathed essence from on high,
  A heaven-lit spark! that could not die.

Not dead — but free — he soars above
  The limit of our lesser scope,

And we, because we shared his love,
  May cherish the uplifting hope
That life to us is more, by just
His altitude above our dust.
  More by the power he has attained
    To minister as angels may;
  More by the knowledge he has gained
    Of love's supremest, patient way;
  Of blessing through the cloud or sun,
  So one all-perfect Will be done.
  And he (the thought is radiant) he
    This very moment may be near,
  With solace meted soothingly
    To feed a hope or hush a fear:
  So true it is, divinest things
  Come borne to us on hidden wings.

  So well we knew our Father's care
    Hovers about us, night and day,
  So sweet it is to think the air
    Is moved in a mysterious way
  By breath of one beloved on earth
  Grown lovelier by celestial birth.
  Then say not he is of the dead,
    'Tis only we in cerements dim,
  Who fail of life around, o'erhead;
    But say it nevermore of him
  Whom death to livelier joys has called,
  Who lives among us disenthralled.

                  Mary B. Dodge.

The Conqueror's Grave.

Within this lowly grave a conqueror lies,
And yet the monument proclaims it not.
    A simple name alone,
    To the great world unknown,
Is graven here, and wild-flowers rising round,
Meek meadow-sweet, and violets of the ground,
    Lean lovingly against the humble stone.

Here in the quiet earth, they laid apart
  No man of iron mould and bloody hands,
But one of tender spirit and delicate frame;
    Gentlest in mien and mind
    Of gentle womankind,
Timidly shrinking from the breath of blame:
One in whose eyes the smile of kindness made
Its haunt, like flowers by sunny brooks in May;
  Yet at the thought of others' pain a shade
Of sweeter sadness chased the smile away.

Nor deem that when the hand that moulders here
Was raised in menace, realms were chilled with fear.
Not thus were waged the mighty wars that gave
The victory to her who fills this grave:
    Alone her task was wrought,
    Alone the battle fought;
Through that long strife her constant hope was staid
On God alone, nor looked for other aid.

She met the hosts of Sorrow with a look
  That altered not beneath the frown they wore,
And soon the lowering brood were tamed, and took,
  Meekly, her gentle rule and frowned no more.
Her soft hand put aside the assaults of wrath,
    And calmly broke in twain
    The fiery shafts of pain,
And rent the nets of passion from her path.
  By that victorious hand dispair was slain;
With love she vanquished hate and overcame
  Evil with good in her great Master's name.

O gentle sleeper, from thy grave I go
  Consoled, though sad, in hope and yet in fear.
    Brief is the time, I know,
    The warfare scarce begun;
Yet all may win the triumphs thou hast won.
  Still flows the fount whose waters strengthened thee;
The victors' names are yet too few to fill
  Heaven's mighty roll; the glorious armory,
That ministered to thee, is open still. *William C. Bryant.*

PART V.

CHILDHOOD — YOUTH.

Sowing in Tears.

Straight and still the baby lies,
No more smiling in his eyes,
Neither tears nor wailing cries.

Smiles and tears alike are done;
He has need of neither one —
Only, I must weep alone.

Tiny fingers, all too slight,
Hold within their grasping tight,
Waxen berries scarce more white.

Nights and days of weary pain
I have held them close — in vain;
Now I never shall again.

Crossed upon a silent breast,
By no suffering distressed,
Here they lie in marble rest.

They shall ne'er unfolded be,
Never more in agony
Cling so pleadingly to me.

Yearning sore, I only know
I am very full of woe —
And I want my baby so!

Weary heart, that thou should'st prove
So unworthy of the love
Which thy darling doth remove!

PART IV.

SUFFERING AND REST.

The Sleep.

" He giveth His beloved sleep." Ps. cxxvii : 2.

Of all the thoughts of God that are
Borne inward unto souls afar,
Along the Psalmist's music deep,
  Now tell me if that any is,
  For gift or grace, surpassing this —
" He giveth his beloved, sleep " ?

What would we give to our beloved ?
The hero's heart to be unmoved,
The poet's star-tuned harp to sweep,
  The patriot's voice to teach and rouse,
  The monarch's crown to light the brows ?
" He giveth his beloved, sleep."

What do we give to our beloved ?
A little faith all undisproved,
A little dust to overweep,
  And bitter memories to make
  The whole earth blasted for our sake.
" He giveth his beloved, sleep."

" Sleep soft, beloved ! " we sometimes say,
But have no tune to charm away
Sad dreams that through the eyelids creep ;
  But never doleful dream again
  Shall break the happy slumber, when
  " He giveth his beloved, sleep."

Sleep, lovely one, sleep!
Earth's beauty is a summer sunset's glow,
Fading to darkness as the night shades grow;
Thy beauty was of climes we do not know.
Sleep, lovely one, sleep!

Sleep, loving one, sleep!
Warm hearts and tender cluster, true and kind;
Thy sorrowing ones they shall not fail to find;
Love well shall guard the love thou leav'st behind.
Sleep, loving one, sleep!

Sleep, beloved one, sleep!
That only asks to rest,
Unquestioning, upon
A loving breast.

My good right hand forgets
Its cunning now;
To march the weary march
I know not how.

He sees when their footsteps falter, when their hearts grow weak and
faint;
He marks when their strength is failing, and listens to each com-
plaint;
He bids them rest for a season, for the path-way has grown too steep;
And folded in fair green pastures, he giveth his loved ones sleep.

Like weary and worn-out children, that sigh for the daylight's close,
He knows that they oft are longing for home and its sweet repose;
So he calls them in from their labors ere the shadows around them
creep,
And silently watching o'er them, he giveth his loved ones sleep.

Be good! and you shall find her where
   No wind can shake the wee bird's nest;
   No dreams can break the wee bird's rest'
No night, no pain, no parting there!

No echoes of old storms gone by!
   Earth's sorrows slumber peacefully;
   The weary are at rest, and He
Shall wipe the tears from every eye.

Gerald Massey.

An Infant's Death.

A snow-flake falls, from out the air above,
Upon some spot of ground where lingers yet
The warmth of Summer's and of Autumn's sun;
And in a moment it has passed from sight.
Most beautiful its crystal shape, a six-
Rayed star, well fitted, if it could have stayed
Until the sunlight fell thereon, to give
A wealth of rainbow-hues, to gladden all
Who saw its loveliness. Why came the flake
Of snow, to go so soon, and leave no trace?
A useless birth, a useless death, it seems.

So seems — but when we trace the snow-flake back,
And try to image all the wondrous store
Of nature's skill in that one bit displayed,
And know how all things joined together are,
And work in harmony in this great world,
So that from furthest parts the forces come,
Which meet an instant, give the snow-flake birth,
Then pass to other work — we know what seems
A trifling thing, is far from being so;
In one grand thought the truth comes home to us,
That, were it not the snow-flake came to earth,
The world could not have been the same to-day.

"Shall I have naught that is fair?" saith he;
  "Have naught but the bearded grain?
Though the breath of these flowers is sweet to me,
  I will give them all back again."

He gazed at the flowers with tearful eyes,
  He kissed their drooping leaves;
It was for the Lord of Paradise
  He bound them in his sheaves.

"My Lord has need of these flowerets gay,"
  The Reaper said, and smiled;
"Dear tokens of the earth are they,
  Where he was once a child."

"They shall all bloom in fields of light,
  Transplanted by my care,
And saints upon their garments white,
  These sacred blossoms wear."

And the mother gave, in tears and pain,
  The flowers she most did love;
She knew she should find them all again
  In the fields of light above.

Oh, not in cruelty, not in wrath,
  The Reaper came that day;
'Twas an angel visited the green earth,
  And took the flowers away.

                              H. W. Longfellow.

The Alpine Sheep.

As this this
~~After our~~ child's untroubled breath
  Up to the Father ~~took~~ its way,
And on ~~our~~ home the shade of death
  Like a long twilight haunting day;

And friends came round, with *their* ~~us~~ to weep
  (Her) little spirit's swift remove,—
The story of the Alpine sheep
  ~~Was told to us by one we love.~~
I tell to thee in tones of love.

They, in the valley's sheltering care,
　Soon crop the meadow's tender prime,
And when the sod grows brown and bare
　The shepherd strives to make them climb

To airy shelves of pastures green,
　That hang along the mountain's side,
Where grass and flowers together lean,
　And down through mists the sunbeams slide.

But nought can tempt the timid things
　The steep and rugged path to try,
Though sweet the shepherd calls and sings,
　And seared below the pastures lie, —

Till in his arms their lambs he takes,
　Along the dizzy verge to go,
Then, heedless of the rifts and breaks,
　They follow on, o'er rock and snow.

And in those pastures, lifted fair,
　More dewy soft than lowland mead,
The shepherd drops his tender care,
　And sheep and lambs together feed.

This parable, by nature breathed,
　Blew on me as the south wind free
O'er frozen brooks, that flow unsheathed
　From icy thraldom to the sea.

A blissful vision, through the night,
　Would all my happy senses sway,
Of the good shepherd on the height,
　Or climbing up the stony way,

Holding a little lamb asleep,
　While, like the murmur of the sea,
Sounded that voice along the deep,
　Saying " Arise, and follow me ! "

　　　　　　　　　Maria Lowell.

Little Children

In the baron's hall of pride,
By the poor man's dull fireside,
'Mid the mighty, 'mid the mean,
Little children may be seen,
Like the flowers that spring up fair,
Bright and countless everywhere!

Blessings on them! they in me
Move a kindly sympathy,
With their wishes, hopes and fears;
With their laughter and their tears;
With their wonder so intense,
And their small experience!

Little children, not alone
On this wide earth are ye known;
'Mid its labors and its cares,
'Mid its sufferings and its snares;
Free from sorrow, free from strife,
In the world of love and life,
Where no sinful thing hath trod —
In the presence of your God,
Spotless, blameless, glorified —
Little children, ye abide.

Mary Howitt.

Buried To-Day.

Buried to-day;
　When the soft green buds are bursting out,
　And up on the south-wind comes a shout
Of village boys and girls at play
In the mild spring evening gray.

Taken away;
　Sturdy of heart and stout of limb,
　From eyes that drew half their light from him,
And put low, low underneath the clay,
In his spring, — on this spring day.

Passes away,
  All the pride of boy-life begun,
  All the hope of life yet to run;
Who dares to question when One saith "Nay."
Murmur not, — only pray

Enters to-day,
  Another body in church-yard sod,
  Another soul on the life in God.
His Christ was buried — and lives alway;
Trust him and go your way.

D. M. Mulock-Craik.

The Changeling.

I had a little daughter,
  And she was given to me
To lead me gently backward
  To the heavenly Father's knee,
That I by the force of nature,
  Might, in some dim wise, divine
The depth of his infinite patience
  To this wayward soul of mine.

I know not how others saw her,
  But to me she was wholly fair,
And the light of the heaven she came from
  Still lingered and gleamed in her hair;
For it was as wavy and golden,
  And as many changes took,
As the shadows of sun-gilt ripples
  On the yellow bed of a brook.

She had been with us scarce a twelvemonth,
  And it hardly seemed a day,
When a troop of wandering angels
  Stole my little daughter away;
Or perhaps those heavenly guardians
  But loosed the hampering strings,
And when they had opened her cage door
  My little bird used her wings.

But they left in her stead a changeling,
 A little angel child,
That seems like a bud in full blossom,
 And smiles as she never smiled.
This child is not mine as the first was,
 I cannot sing it to rest,
I cannot lift it up fatherly
 And bliss it upon my breast ;
Yet it lies in my little one's cradle,
 And sits in my little one's chair,
And the light of the heaven she's gone to
 Transfigures its golden hair.

      J. R. Lowell.

The Chamber Over the Gate.

Is it so far from thee
Thou canst no longer see,
In the Chamber over the Gate,
That old man desolate,
Weeping and wailing sore
For his son, who is no more?
 O Absalom, my son!

Is it so long ago
That cry of human woe
From the walled city came,
Calling on his dear name,
That it has died away
In the distance of to-day?
 O Absalom, my son!

There is no far or near,
There is neither there nor here,
There is neither soon nor late,
In that Chamber over the Gate,
Nor any long ago
To that cry of human woe,
 O Absalom, my son!

Somewhere at every hour
The watchman on the tower
Looks forth, and sees the fleet
Approach of the hurrying feet
Of messengers, that bear
The tidings of despair.
  O Absalom, my son!

He goes forth from the door,
Who shall return no more.
With him our joy departs;
The light goes out in our hearts;
In the Chamber over the Gate
We sit disconsolate.
  O Absalom, my son!

That 't is a common grief
Bringeth but slight relief;
Ours is the bitterest loss,
Ours is the heaviest cross;
And forever the cry will be
" Would God I had died for thee,
  O Absalom, my son!"

                              H. W. Longfellow.

My Child.

I cannot make him dead!
His fair sunshiny head
Is ever bounding round my study chair;
Yet when my eyes, now dim
With tears, I turn to him,
The vision vanishes, — he is not there!

I walk my parlor floor,
And, through the open door,
I hear a footfall on the chamber stair;
I 'm stepping toward the hall
To give the boy a call;
And then bethink me that — he is not there!

I know his face is hid
  Under the coffin lid,
Closed are his eyes; cold is his forehead fair;
  My hand that marble felt;
  O'er it in prayer I knelt;
Yet my heart whispers that — he is not there!

  Not there!   Where, then, is he?
  The form I used to see
Was but the raiment that he used to wear.
  The grave, that now doth press
  Upon that cast-off dress,
Is but his wardrobe locked; he is not there!

  He lives! — in all the past
  He lives; nor to the last,
Of seeing him again will I despair;
  In dreams I see him now;
  And, on his angel brow,
I see it written, " Thou shalt see me *there!* "

  Yes, we all live to God!
  Father, thy chastening rod
So help us, thine afflicted ones, to bear,
  That, in the spirit land,
  Meeting at thy right hand,
'Twill be our heaven to find that — he is there.

                  John Pierpont.

The Morning-Glory.

We wreathed about our darling's head
  The morning-glory bright;
Her little face looked out beneath
  So full of life and light,
So lit, as with a sunrise,
  That we could only say,
"She is the morning-glory true,
  And her poor types are they."

So always from that happy time
　　We called her by their name,
And very fitting did it seem, —
　　For, sure as morning came,
Behind her cradle bars she smiled
　　To catch the first faint ray,
As from the trellis smiles the flower,
　　And opens to the day.

We used to think how she had come,
　　Even as comes the flower,
The last and perfect added gift
　　To crown Love's morning hour;
And how in her was imaged forth
　　The love we could not say,
As on the little dewdrops round
　　Shines back the heart of day.

The morning-glory's blossoming
　　Will soon be coming round, —
We see their rows of heart-shaped leaves
　　Upspringing from the ground;
The tender things the winter killed
　　Renew again their birth,
But the glory of our morning
　　Has passed away from earth.

Earth! in vain our aching eyes
　　Stretch over thy green plain!
Too harsh thy dews, too gross thine air,
　　Her spirit to sustain;
But up in groves of Paradise
　　Full surely we shall see
Our morning-glory beautiful
　　Twine round our dear Lord's knee.

Maria Lowell.

For when the morn came dim and sad,
  And chill with early showers,
Her quiet eyelids closed, — she had
  Another morn than ours.

Thomas Hood.

The Lent Jewels.

In schools of wisdom all the day was spent;
His steps at eve the Rabbi homeward bent,
With homeward thoughts which dwelt upon the wife
And two fair children who consoled his life:
She, meeting at the threshold, led him in,
And with the words preventing did begin, —
" Ever rejoicing at your wished return,
Yet do I most so now; for since this morn
I have been much perplexed and sorely tried
Upon one point which you shall now decide.

" Some years ago a friend into my care
Some jewels gave; rich precious gems they were;
But having given them in my charge, this friend
Did afterward nor come for them nor send,
But left them in my keeping for so long
That now it almost seems to me a wrong
That he should suddenly arrive to-day
To take those jewels which he left, away.
What think you ?   Shall I freely yield them back,
And with no murmuring — so henceforth to lack
Those gems myself, which I had learned to see
Almost as mine forever, mine in fee ? "
" What question can be here ?   Your own true heart
Must needs advise you of the only part;
That may be claimed again which was but lent,
And should be yielded without discontent;
Nor surely can we find herein a wrong,
That it was left us to enjoy it long."

"Good is the word," she answered. "May we now
And evermore that it is good allow!"
And rising, to an inner chamber led,
And there she showed him, stretched upon one bed,
Two children pale ; and he the jewels knew
Which God had lent him and resumed anew.

R. C. Trench.

Resignation.

There is no flock, however watched and tended,
  But one dead lamb is there !
There is no fireside, howsoe'er defended,
  But has one vacant chair !

The air is full of farewells to the dying,
  And mournings for the dead ;
The heart of Rachel, for her children crying,
  Will not be comforted !

Let us be patient ! These severe afflictions
  Not from the ground arise,
But oftentimes celestial benedictions
  Assume this dark disguise.

We see but dimly through the mists and vapors ;
  Amid these earthly damps,
What seem to us but sad, funereal tapers
  May be heaven's distant lamps.

There is no Death ! What seems so is transition ;
  This life of mortal breath
Is but a suburb of the life elysian,
  Whose portal we call Death.

She is not dead, — the child of our affection, —
  But gone unto that school
Where she no longer needs our poor protection,
  And Christ himself doth rule.

In that great cloister's stillness and seclusion,
  By guardian angels led,
Safe from temptation, safe from sin's pollution,
  She lives, whom we call dead.

Day after day, we think what she is doing
  In those bright realms of air;
Year after year, her tender steps pursuing,
  Behold her grown more fair.

Thus do we walk with her, and keep unbroken
  The bonds which nature gives,
Thinking that our remembrance, though unspoken,
  May reach her where she lives.

Not as a child shall we again behold her;
  For, when with raptures wild
In our embraces we again enfold her,
  She will not be a child,

But a fair maiden, in her Father's mansion,
  Clothed with celestial grace;
And beautiful with all the soul's expansion
  Shall we behold her face.

And though, at times, impetuous with emotion
  And anguish long suppressed,
The swelling heart heaves, moaning like the ocean
  That cannot be at rest, —

We will be patient, and assuage the feeling
  We may not wholly stay;
By silence sanctifying, not concealing,
  The grief that must have way.

                H. W. Longfellow.

Vesta.

O Christ of God! whose life and death
  Our own have reconciled,
Most quietly, most tenderly,
  Take home this little child!

Thy grace is in her patient eyes,
  Thy words are on her tongue;
The very silence round her seems
  As if the angels sung.

Her smile is as a listening child's
  Who hears its mother call ;
The lilies of thy perfect peace
  About her pillow fall.

She leans from out our clinging arms
  To rest herself in thine;
Alone to thee, dear Lord, can we
  Our well-beloved resign !

Oh, less for her than for ourselves
  We bow our heads and pray;
Her setting star, like Bethlehem's
  To thee shall point the way.

                              J. G. Whittier.

Lifted Over.

As tender mothers guiding baby steps,
Where places come at which the tiny feet
Would trip, lift up the little ones in arms
Of love, and set them down beyond the harm,
So did our Father watch the precious boy,
Led o'er the stones by me, who stumbled oft
Myself, but strove to help my darling on :
He saw the sweet limbs faltering, and saw
Rough ways before us, where my arms would fail;
So reached from heaven, and lifting the dear child,
Who smiled in leaving me, he put him down,
Beyond all hurt, beyond my sight, and bade
Him wait for me !   Shall I not then be glad,
And, thanking God, press on to overtake ?

                              H. H.

INDEX OF FIRST LINES.

SUPPLEMENTARY LIST OF POEMS.

Reference is made to the following books : —

Putnam. Singers and Songs of the Liberal Faith. [Boston. Roberts.
Schaff & Gilman. Library of Religious Poetry. [N. Y. 1881.
Quiet Hours. 2 vols. [Boston. Roberts.
Bryant. Library of Poetry and Song. [N. Y. 1872
Chadwick, J. W. Poems. [Boston. Roberts.
Household Edition — Poems of Longfellow, Whittier, Lowell, Bryant, Alice
   and Phœbe Cary. [Boston, Houghton, Mifflin & Co.
Sunshine in the Soul. 2 vols. [Boston. Roberts.
Hymns of the Ages. 3 vols. [Boston. Houghton, Mifflin & Co.
Revised Hymn & Tune Book. [Boston. Amer. Unitarian Association.
Memory and Hope. [Boston. Ticknor & Fields. 1851
Sunday Book of Praise. Golden Treasury Series. [London. Macmillan.
Proctor, A. A. Poems. [Boston. 1880.
Verses, by " H. H." [Boston. Roberts.
Sursum Corda. [Boston. Roberts. 1877
Hosmer and Gannett. The Thought of God. [Boston. Roberts. 1885
Brooks, C. T. Memoir and Poems. [Boston. Roberts. 1885
Hemans, F. Poems. [Boston. 1833.
Lyra Americana. [N. Y. 1865.
Shadow of the Rock. [N. Y. Randolph.
The Changed Cross. " "
Palace of the King. " "
The Chamber of Peace. " "
Uplands of God. " "
Cheering Words. " "

PART I. — LIFE AND DEATH.

FUNERAL HYMN . . . . *W. R. Alger.*
   "The worlds that shine above us nightly."
                                    Putnam, 471
PRAYER AND THE DEAD . . . . *N. L. Frothingham.*
   "They passed away from sight and hands."
                     Putnam. 102. Quiet Hours, I., 149.
MORTAL AND IMMORTAL . . . . *R. C. Watterson.*
   " I stand between the Future and the Past."
                     Schaff & Gilman, 302. Putnam, 403

218   SUPPLEMENTARY POEMS.

PART III. — A GOOD LIFE.

"GO TO THE GRAVE IN ALL THY GLORIOUS PRIME."
Montgomery.
Rev. H. & T. Book, 756 ⌐

TRIBUTE TO BISHOP HEBER . . . *Mrs. Hemans.*
"If it be sad to speak of treasures gone."
(A wise and useful man.)   Poems, B. 1833, I., 187

PART IV. — SUFFERING — REST.

∨ DECORATION . . . . . *T. W. Higginson.*
"'Mid the flower-wreathed tombs I stand."
Scribner's Monthly, June, 1874. Putnam, 483
(For a woman heroic in suffering.)

RESTING IN HOPE . . . . *H. Bonar.*
"Rest for the toiling hand."
Rev. H. & T. Book, 702 ⌐

BEAR OUT THE DEAD . . . . . *Haven.*
"Ay, carry out your dead."
Schaff & Gilman, 886

REST . . . . *Euphemia Saxby.*
"It was Thy will, my Father."
Quiet Hours, I., 144

∨ THE GATE OF HEAVEN . . . . *Disciples Hymn Book.*
"She stood outside the gate of Heaven."
(For an ill life.)   Quiet Hours, I., 162

∨ "AH, WELL! SHE HAD HER WILL."
Sursum Corda, 279
(For one who suffered secretly, and was misunderstood.)

∨ ON HIS BLINDNESS . . . . . . *Milton.*
(For one blind.)

"THOU KNOWEST, LORD, THE WEARINESS AND SORROW."
Jane Borthwick.
Sursum Corda, 30

∨ FROM "MIRIAM." . . . . . . *Whittier.* —
"Wherever through the ages rise the altars of self-sacrifice."
Poems, 342

"GOING HOME." . . . . . . *Anonymous.*
"'Heimgang!' So the German people."
(For a German family.)   Uplands of God, 53 —

∨ THE SWEET SURPRISE. (In part.) . . . *Anonymous.*
"Down to the borders of the silent land."
(For one who lingered.)   Uplands of God, 69 —

PART V. — CHILDHOOD — YOUTH.

PART VI. — OLD AGE.

O THOU before whose sight all generations of men pass over to their rest, to thee alone can we turn in this hour. Amid all life's changes thou art the same forever, and thy years shall have no end.   Thou art the source of all life.   Thou art the Power above all powers and Lord of Death.   To thee we come, who dost clothe the grass of the field, and mark the falling sparrow.   To thy unfailing compassion we look, thou who dost note thy children's pain and grief.   We bring these empty hearts, this loneliness, this sorrow, and lay them at thy feet. Thou knowest it all, our Father, and because thou knowest, canst help us.   Comfort us with thy love, greater than a mother's love for her child!   Send thy pity to lighten the darkness; send thy patience that we may bear this trial bravely.   Touch these wounds with thy hand of healing, and help us to be still.

Almighty Father, give us of thy strength that we may take up our lives more bravely for the sake of this dear one who has now done with earth.   May we learn to be faithful in duty, thoughtful, tender of others, loyal to the service of holiness and truth, because of those who can work no longer here on earth.   May we think not of our loss, our suffering, but of their release, of the peace that rests upon this mortal body, and the freedom wherein the soul has now found a higher joy.

Grant, we pray thee, the faith that these ties of affection — the holiest thing thou givest us to know — can never perish.   Wheresoever this dear friend may go, he can not be forgetful of us, and henceforth we are no more strangers to the life beyond since these have entered to make it home.

Now, Almighty Creator, into thy hands we commend

the spirit thou didst give. We thank thee for the memory of his life. No longer can we care for him ; but thou wilt care for him better than our love could do. By pastures green and by quiet waters, into new realms of purity and love and truth, into new and higher labors in thy service thou wilt lead him. Cherish and keep him, we pray thee, and through ways unknown to us bring him at last nearer to thy Presence, O God of the Living and the Dead !

And when we, too, are called to bid farewell to this world of love and beauty, of joy and sorrow, grant that we may follow after him. Grant that our love may grow stronger in these years of absence. Bring us, if it be thy purpose with us, bring us together again where we may know each other better. May we trust the highest instincts of this human heart, telling us that the love which conquers death is forever immortal. We ask in the memory of Jesus, our Elder Brother. In memory of his tender heart, his courage and purity, we would be lifted up into his peace, and learn with him to pray : Thy will, not ours, O God ! Thou didst give, and thou hast taken away. Blessed be the name of the Lord !

C. J. S.

O THOU who art the Beginning and the End of all lives, in whom the living live and the dead sleep, grant that we in the presence of death may feel that our true life is in thee. Thou who hast made us as we are made, to love life, and to grieve and suffer in the presence of death, be near to us when we call upon thy name, feeling in that presence we have no help save in thee alone. It is our comfort and consolation in turning our hearts to thee, when they are made heavy by sorrow, that thou art greater than our hearts and knowest all things. When our grief is too great to be uttered, and our need is more and deeper than we know or can express, thou knowest it altogether. Thy hand, Father Almighty, has fashioned the ties that bind us one to another in love and friendship, and when those ties are broken by death, that which we have to suffer is known to thee alone. We desire to feel, though we cannot know that thy will in trouble and affliction is not to punish us but to bless us; that alike in all we are born to suffer in our affections, and in all the happiness and enjoyment we derive from them, the pity and goodness of the Highest are manifested and expressed. We desire in our darkest hours to trust thee, and against doubts and fears that test us and perplex us, to cling to the belief that all is for the best, not meant to crush us or to extinguish our hopes and desires for those we love and for ourselves, but to work out for them and for us good beyond our belief and hope.

When our faith is weak, and heart and flesh faint and fail, good Lord, have mercy upon us; in thy mercy remember us; in thy pity visit us, that in the thought of thy pity we may be saved from despair of ourselves. Thou knowest how hard it is for us to assure ourselves, when those we love better than life are taken from us, that we are not forgotten or disowned by Him that made us, that our loss is not all loss, and our suffering and anguish not all vain and fruitless. Our affections cling to that which is earthly and familiar to us, so that it is hard for us to think and feel that our beloved dead whose faces we shall no more behold, are still with thee and that in thy presence and dominion death hath n more dominion over them.

Like as a father pitieth his children, so the Lord pitieth them that fear him. Even as we are moved by pity for the weak, and downcast, and sorrowful, so our hearts assure us it must be that He who is the highest of all must be the best of all, pitiful and compassionate beyond our belief and hope, to all that lives and breathes.

Grant, our Father, that we may in all trouble that is darkest and deepest, find in this revelation of thyself within us, thy consolation ministered to us, and thy light lightening our darkness.

Help of all the sorrowful, Comforter of all that mourn, we remember in thy presence those whose share in the sorrow we feel this day is heaviest and sorest. Comfort them by the sympathy of friends, and much more by thy grace. Consecrate this sorrow for all of us who have part in it, and grant that even what is darkest and most mysterious in it, may not be without profit in showing us and opening for us the path of life.

We remember in thy presence, now and here, all the children of sorrow, above all those whose sorrow like ours this day, is for the dead, concerning whom their souls refuse to be comforted. In the darkness and mystery in which their lives are shrouded, may light arise for them, and shine upon them from the sympathy of their kind, much more from thee the First and the Last, thou whose tender mercies are over all thy works, who knoweth our frame, who remembereth that we are dust.

JOHN SERVICE.

Why fear death? It is the most beautiful adventure in life.

[Frohman - on sinking of Lusitania] (5/7/15) 168-8

For as much as your dear on[e]
has departed this life we commi[t]
{his}
{her} tabernacle of earth to the care
keeping of mother nature, and
~~commend~~ commit the soul of {him} you love
{her}
to the Father of all souls in th[e su]re
and certain hope of the reunion,
the spiritual nature and life ever
lasting.

———

"Then with no fiery throbs of pain
No cold gradations of decay,
"Death" broke at once the vital cha[in]
And freed {his} soul the nearest w[ay]
       {her}
                    (S. Johnson 170-1[6]

———

"Why should we fear Death,
Who gives us Life and in exchange takes bre[ath]
                    (Knowles

Thots for funerals.

No Death — all is Life.

Death a liberator & broadener.

Love will brook no absence {m &c.

Human Longings — satisfied.

Soul taken a Journey.

Essential Immortality.

Divine Purpose

Removal" — old house — new.

Life is one — same laws for soul.

MIZPAH.

SENT BY MISS LIZZIE S. TURNEY, SOMERVILLE, MASS.

"The Lord watch between me and thee when
we are absent one from another." Gen. 31:9.

Go thou thy way, and I go mine:
   Apart, yet not afar,
Only a thin veil hangs between
   The pathways where we are.
And "God keep watch 'tween thee and me;"
   This is my prayer;
He looks thy way, He looketh mine.
   And keeps us near.

I know not where thy road may lie,
   Or which way mine may be;
If mine will lead thro' parching sands,
   And thine beside the sea;
Yet God keeps watch 'tween thee and me,
   So never fear;
He holds thy hand, He claspeth mine,
   And keeps us near.

There love and light will sure be thine,
Here my lot lowly be;
Your life be full of joy and peace,
And longing be for me;

Yet God keep watch 'tween thee and me,
   Both be His care;
One arm 'round thee, and one 'round me,
   Will keep us near.

I sigh, sometimes, to see thy face,
   But since this may not be,
I leave thee to the care of Him
   Who cares for thee and me.
"I'll keep you both beneath my wings,"
   This comforts, dear:
One wing o'er thee, and one o'er me,
   So are we near.

And tho' our paths be separate,
   And thy way is not mine,
Yet coming to the Mercy Seat,
   My soul will meet with thine,
And "God keep watch 'tween thee and me,"
   I'll whisper there.
He blesseth thee, He blesseth me,
   And keeps us near.
            [JULIA A. BAKER.

Crossing the Bar

Sunset and evening star,
And one clear call for me!
And may there be no moaning of the bar
When I put out to sea.

But such a tide as moving seems asleep
Too full for sound and foam
When that which drew from out the boundless deep
Again turns home.

...ning bell,
...the dark!
...sadness of farewell
...

...our bourne of Time + Place
...bear me far,
...Pilot face to face
...cross the bar.
  A Tennyson

The Meaning of It All.

BY MRS. M. A. KIDDER.

We often sit and wonder
  At the strange things taking place!
Life's ebbing and its flowing—
  The coming and the going
  Of the busy human race.

We are not always willing
  To humbly watch and wait.
To bear our cross of sorrow,
  That a fair crown on the morrow
  May await us at the gate.

Large daily ask the question
  As we taste the cup of gall
  In the midst of care and labor,—
  "What, my friend and neighbor,
  Is the meaning of it all?

"Why is it that we know not,
  As we sow the early seed,
Whether sunbeams will caress it,
  And the dews of heaven bless it,
  With fruition in its need?

"Or whether as it sleepeth,
  Underneath the quickening mold,
The lightning bolt may smite it,
  Or the creeping mildew blight it,
  That it bear no grains of gold?"

We ask, and yet kind Heaven
  Hath taught us all to trust,
(The sowers and the reapers
  All but the idle sleepers),
  And Heaven, we know, is just.

There is a time for all things
  In joy as well as thrall—
And that sweet day is dawning
When we shall know (blest morning!)
  The meaning of it all!

From the Poets

THOUGH LOST TO SIGHT

eetheart, good-bye! the fluttering sail
s spread to waft me far from thee;
d soon before the favoring gale
My ship shall bound the sea.
rchance all desolate and forlorn,
These eyes shall miss thee many a
    year;
t unforgotten every charm—
Though lost to sight, to mem'ry dear.

eetheart, good-bye! one last embrace!
cruel fate, two souls to sever!
t in this heart's most sacred place
Thou, thou alone shall dwell forever.
d still shall recollection trace
In Fancy's mirror ever near,
ch smile, each tear upon that face
Though lost to sight, to mem'ry dear.
RUTHVEN JENHYNS.

BEAUTIFUL THINGS

Beautiful faces are those that wear,
It matters little if dark or fair,
Whole-souled honesty printed there.

Beautiful eyes are those that show
Like crystal panes where hearth-fires glo\
Beautiful thoughts that burn below.

Beautiful lips are those whose words
Leap from the heart like songs of birds
Yet whose utterance prudence girds.

Beautiful hands are those that do
Work that is earnest and brave and true,
Moment by moment the long day through.

Beautiful feet are those that go
On kindly ministries to and fro,
Down lowliest ways if God wills it so.

Beautiful shoulders are those that bear
Ceaseless burdens of homely care,
With patient grace and daily prayer.

Beautiful lives are those that bless
Silent rivers of happiness,
Whose hidden fountains but few may guess.

www.ingramcontent.com/pod-product-compliance
Lightning Source LLC
LaVergne TN
LVHW012202040326
832903LV00003B/78